Radical Criminology

issue four ★ summer/fall 2014

ISSN: 1929-7904
ISBN: 978-0692311417

a publication of the
Critical Criminology Working Group
at Kwantlen Polytechnic University
(12666 72 Avenue, Surrey, BC V3W 2M8)
www.radicalcriminology.org

punctum books ★ brooklyn, ny
www.punctumbooks.com

✶ Radical Criminology ✶ Issue 4 ✶ October 2014 ✶ ISSN 1929-7904

General Editor: Jeff Shantz

Feature Guest Editor: Public Criminology Justin Piché

Production Editor: PJ Lilley

Advisory Board: Olga Aksyutina, Institute for African Studies of Russian Academy of Sciences, Moscow; **Davina Bhandar** (Trent U.); **Jeff Ferrell** (Texas Christian U.); **Hollis Johnson** (Kwantlen Polytechnic U.); **Michael J. Lynch** (U. of South Florida); **Mike CK Ma** (Kwantlen Polytechnic U.); **Lisa Monchalin** (Kwantlen Polytechnic U.); **Heidi Rimke** (U.Winnipeg); **Jeffrey Ian Ross** (U.Baltimore); **Herman Schwendinger**, independent scholar

cover art: Anonymous Joyceville prisoners

Unless otherwise stated, contributions express the opinions of their writers and are not (necessarily) those of the Editors or Advisory Board. Please visit our website for more information.

✶ Contact Us ✶

email: editors@radicalcriminology.org
website: http://journal.radicalcriminology.org
Mailing address: Kwantlen Polytechnic University, ATTN: Jeff Shantz, Dept. of Criminology
12666 72 Avenue | Surrey, BC, Canada V3W 2M8

This work is licensed under the **Creative Commons Attribution- NonCommercial NoDerivs 3.0 Unported License,** enabling non-commercial use, distribution, and reproduction of the published article in any medium, provided that the original work is **properly cited.**
http://creativecommons.org/licenses/by-nc-nd/3.0/
Attribution to include the author or artist's name, date of first publication, and our journal's name, *Radical Criminology*.

✶

Our website uses the Open Journal System, developed by the Public Knowledge Project at Simon Fraser University:

journal.radicalcriminology.org

Here, you may create your own profile to contribute to this project, or simply subscribe your email address to our low traffic mailing list, to receive notifications of important new content added to the journal. Use of your address is limited to matters relating to the journal, and we will not be sharing our subscribers list with other organizations.

✶

As an online, open access publication,
all our content is freely available to all researchers worldwide ensuring maximum dissemination.

✶

Printed paper copies with full color cover
are available at cost through

punctum books ✶ brooklyn, ny

www . punctumbooks . com

"SPONTANEOUS ACTS OF SCHOLARLY COMBUSTION"

[more re: **punctum books**, see pg. 16]

& now introducing...

Thought | Crimes

a new, open access press
from the publishers of **Radical Criminology**,
& an imprint of
punctum books * brooklyn, ny

with our first book, a stunning historical memoir...

WHO KILLED THE BERKELEY SCHOOL? Struggles over Radical Criminology

by
Herman & Julia Schwendinger

234 pages.
ISBN: 0615990932

Now available in paperback or download it as a PDF or EPUB free...

thoughtcrimespress . org

Inside

editorial /

7) Going Forth
Jeff Shantz

features > public criminology

11) Critical Reflections on 'Public Criminology': An Introduction
Justin Piché, Guest Editor

17) Public Criminology in the Cold City: Engagement and Possibility
Andrew Woolford & Bryan Hogeveen

37) The Public Would Rather Watch Hockey! The Promises and Institutional Challenges of *'Doing'* Public Criminology within the Academy
Carrie B. Sanders & Lauren Eisler

67) Troubling Publics: A Feminist Analysis of Public Criminology
Amanda Nelund

85) On Some Limits and Paradoxes of Academic Orations on Public Criminology
Nicolas Carrier

arts /

115) Prisoner's Justice Day, a retrospective compiled by **pj lilley**

149) *Seeking Justice for Missing and Murdered Native Women* **a poem by Lisa Monchalin**

insurgencies /

155) Anarchism: A critical analysis. **Christopher Howell**

book reviews /

165) *The Struggle Within: Prisons, Political Prisoners, and Mass Movements in the United States* (Dan Berger) Reviewed by—**Jordan House**

170) *Killer Weed: Marijuana Grow Ops, Media, and Justice* (Dr. Susan Boyd and Dr. Connie Carter) Reviewed by—**Charles Reasons**

Editorial:
Going Forth

Welcome to the fourth issue of *Radical Criminology*. We hope you find it interesting and instigating. We began this project two years ago with a conviction about the need for a venue for the expression of radical perspectives in criminology and a commitment to bring together criminologists of the schools and of the streets in a common space. The great positive response to, and support for, the journal has been quite phenomenal. We have received notes of appreciation and encouragement from people on every continent. We have heard from academics and activists, criminologists and community organizers, alike. It has emphatically confirmed and deepened our belief that there is a substantial pressing need for venues for radical criminological analysis and agitation in the current period of law and order austerity and repression.

Release of the fourth issue of a journal is a particularly gratifying event. The first issue is always accompanied by anticipatory excitement and hopefulness. But publishing graveyards are filled with wonderful journals that only survived for one issue. A second issue is cause for celebration to be sure but can still hold a threat of being flukey. The fourth issue suggests the journal has some staying power and is on a good footing. This is especially true in this case given the growing numbers and continuing high quality of submissions.

There have also been some notable occurrences along the way. Christopher Petrella's article "The Color of Corporate Corrections" was profiled in numerous major mass media outlets, including *Mother Jones*, *USA Today*, Tavis Smiley, and Bill Moyers. It has had a real impact on understandings of an issue of great importance.

Events that occurred over the period of this issue's production reinforced, rather starkly, the necessity for an active, publicly engaged criminology rooted in radical and insurgent perspectives, practices, and movements. A criminology that asserts radical visions openly and unflinchingly is as important as ever. One of the painfully telling events was the police murder, execution really, of an unarmed African American teenager, Mike Brown, in Ferguson, Missouri, and subsequently the military response to, and violence inflicted upon, community members who took to the streets to express their grief and anger over the police killing and the lack of sanction on the officer responsible. The ongoing militarization of police forces in North America, not only in terms of weaponry, armor, vehicles, and munitions but in the development and treatment of "hostiles" (members of the public) was certainly brought to the forefront of public consciousness. It very much appeared that the police in Ferguson viewed themselves and acted as an occupying force.

Another, also troubling issue, was revealed, with less comment, by the response to the Ferguson execution. That was the reliance of the corporate mass media on (ex)cop criminologists for comment and "analysis" (excuse). Various (ex)cop criminologists were put forward to discuss the case and without exception they legitimized, justified, and explain away the murder of Mike Brown by their (former) colleagues. "You don't know what it's like out there." People don't always stop when shot the first time." Such attempts at legitimation, disgusting and contemptible, relied on the credibility afforded by the designation "criminologist." They put the discipline at service as apologists for extrajudicial state murder.

As we bring out an issue on public criminology it is important to recognize and address this. Not all public criminology is radical, critical, or even simply honorable. Radical criminology must find ways to get our perspectives out in the world. Whether that is through journals, editorials, blogs, or websites or through means like twitter (where most of the best analysis of Ferguson occurred and/or was circulated). We have developed @critcrim on twitter as well as a RadicalCriminology Youtube channel.

Another issue related to the state apologist criminology after Ferguson that requires some note is the number of often acting cops fancying themselves as criminologists and getting hired by criminology departments (focused on labor market ready education, job preparation, and "results" oriented funding formulas). Indeed there are now developing entire dedicated professional programs, mostly online or through limited residencies, offering advanced credentials to police officers cum criminologists. Universities in England, for example, are giving out Prof Docs to cops who need the designation to jump a pay grade in the force. Unwary criminology departments are treating these as earned academic doctorates for purposes of hiring. Given the status and legitimacy of officers with local media, and the further boost in status and credibility provided by their professorial status, it is a real possibility that these will increasingly be the faces of public criminology within mass media outlets.

This is our first guest edited volume and we thank Justin Piché for his diligent and enthusiastic work in seeing the public criminology section through production. Several more guest edited volumes are on the way as the journal increasingly becomes a community resource for criminologists and activists alike who are striving for an insurgent criminology, a criminology of resistance.

We would also like to thank all of the folks who have signed up on our Open Journal Systems website, some of whom we have contacted for upcoming reviews. And if you haven't heard from us, please don't hesitate to log in or drop us an email, and please do not forget to add your list of areas of interest/study to your profile so that we can request your comments (or request your participation in our blind peer review process) on future submissions.

Jeff Shantz
Surrey

JEFF SHANTZ, AUGUST 2014,
SURREY, B.C. (UNCEDED COAST SALISH TERRITORIES)

[features: PUBLIC CRIMINOLOGY]

Critical Reflections on 'Public Criminology': An Introduction

JUSTIN PICHÉ, EDITOR
(UNIVERSITY OF OTTAWA)

Currently, there are a number of disciplines in the social sciences where a "public turn" (Nickel 2010, 698) is being advocated. When one calls upon other scholars to 'go public' they are usually asking their colleagues to move beyond what is imagined to be their comfort zones, to do what is allegedly unusual, and engage publics beyond their university classrooms and other academic forums to impact social change concerning the substantive topics addressed in their research. These clarion calls are often set against a contextual backdrop where the world is thought to have just recently gone to shit due to populist politics, mass ignorance and lack of exposure to, or adherence to the lessons found within, academic studies. The proposed antidote offered by proponents of public social sciences often comes in the form of cold, hard 'truths' that scholars are claimed to be well-positioned to provide, but too often fail to effectively communicate because of the narrow scope of publics they normally engage.

In criminology, engagement with extra-academic publics has been the focus of a number of recent works published in academic venues including, but not limited to, scholarly journal issues (e.g. Chancer and McLaughlin 2007; Gies and Mawby

2009; Clear 2010; Loader and Sparks 2011a) and books (e.g. Loader and Sparks 2011b). A common starting point of contemporary calls for a 'public criminology' is the observation that the discipline is a "successful failure", which is gaining more clout in the academic world as evidenced by such things as the creation of new criminology programs in universities, while its agenda setting influence in other spheres is diminishing (ibid, 11). This gripe is long-standing and has animated previous calls for criminologists to get more involved in debates about 'crime' and its repression beyond the academy (e.g. Carrabine *et al.* 2000; Garland and Sparks 2000).

Proponents of 'public criminology' (e.g. Currie 2007; Uggen and Inderbitzin 2010), or what Carlen (2012, 17) calls "doing politics" in criminology, generally focus on three issues. A primary thrust of their deliberations is focused on the objectives of 'public criminology', which are primarily the pursuit of relevance beyond the academy to ensure the discipline's survival going forward and to have an impact on public opinion, as well as policy and practice concerning 'crime-control'. A second aspect of the debate aims to identify the extra-academic publics of criminology, who tend to be politicians, policy makers and the general public. A third issue addressed in these exchanges is the matter of practice, which most often takes the form of policy work (e.g. Stanko 2007), newsmaking criminology (e.g. Barak 2007) and public education (e.g. Currie 2007), or a combination of the three (e.g. Piché forthcoming). Critical reflections on the objectives, publics and practices of 'public criminology' have also emerged raising questions such as whether the pursuit of relevance corrupts academic independence and undermines the possibility for critical research (e.g. Carlen, 2012). Others are sceptical of the idea that engaging powerful actors on their turf can operate as a form of trickle-down criminology, which benefits the marginalized by generating initiatives that concretely reduce the repression they experience and effectively address their material needs (e.g. Ruggiero, 2012).

While the literature on 'public criminology' continues to grow, with few exceptions (e.g. Mopas and Moore, 2012) Canadian scholars have remained on the margins of this discussion. It is with this in mind that a stream of sessions featuring papers on 'public criminology' in Canada were organized as part of the *Critical Perspectives: Criminology and Social Justice—Third National Conference* (CP3) held in May 2013. Since 2011, this annual conference, which takes place at the University of Ottawa and Carleton University on a rotating basis, brings together criminologists from across the country and elsewhere in the world to share research that critically examines domination in all of its guises. This special issue of *Radical Criminology* includes selected papers from the conference that push and/or challenge the boundaries of what is considered to be 'public criminology'.

The collection begins with an auto-ethnographic account by Andrew Woolford and Bryan Hogeveen, entitled "Public Criminology in the Cold City: Engagement and Possibility", that critically reflects on their past involvement in non-profit organizations who work with criminalized persons. Their article, which includes examples of incidents where the imperatives of organizational survival were put before all else, raises questions about the limits of social justice work within entities that are integral to, and/or subject to the demands of, increasingly repressive states under neo-liberalism.

Shifting the conversation from beyond the realm of the academy to the machinations of the university, "The Public Would Rather Watch Hockey! The Promises and Institutional Challenges of 'Doing' Public Criminology within the Academy" by Carrie B. Sanders and Lauren Eisler explores the structural forces they encountered during the development of a course designed to expose students and residents of their community to criminological research. Their experience, particularly as it relates to the search for funding to support their initiative, highlights both the opportunities and constraints shaping 'public criminology' initiatives within increasingly corporate and managerial universities.

To date, it is curious to see the work of radical criminologists rarely mentioned in the discussion on 'public criminology'. Among them are the contributions of feminist criminologists involved in struggles to fight gender, sexual and other forms of inequality. In "Troubling Publics: A Feminist Analysis of Public Criminology", Amanda Nelund discusses how feminism can address key limitations of 'public criminology' as it relates to its approach to the production and dissemination of knowledge, which she argues currently limits its ability to affect fundamental social change.

This issue concludes with an article by Nicolas Carrier entitled "On Some Limits and Paradoxes of Academic Orations of Public Criminology". In this piece, the author identifies numerous pitfalls with the kinds of 'public criminology' championed in the literature and, similarly to Ruggiero (2012), proposes that civic engagement amongst criminologists on matters of (in)justice should be based on solidarity with others, rather than the 'truths' constructed in academic work.

To conclude, I would like to thank those who contributed to this project and made it possible, beginning with the presenters and participants who attended the sessions on 'public criminology' at CP3. Your remarks and questions pushed the discussion on public engagement in criminology in novel directions, which is reflected in the articles included in this issue. I would also like to thank the reviewers, who took the time to comment on the submissions considered for this collection, for their thorough and thoughtful feedback. Lastly, I wish to acknowledge the efforts of the editorial team at *Radical Criminology* who supported this project throughout the process, and continue the work required to maintain a quality peer-reviewed and open journal that is accessible to all with Internet access. This journal is an example of 'public criminology' in action and the articles in this collection offer important insights that will inform how intellectuals think about and engage with publics within and beyond the academia to fight for social justice in our world going forward.

References

Barak, G. (2007). Doing Newsmaking Criminology From Within the Academy. *Theoretical Criminology*, 11(2), 191-207.

Carlen, P. (2012). Criminological Knowledge: Doing Critique; Doing Politics, in S. Hall & S. Winlow (Eds.), *New Directions in Criminological Theory* (pp. 17-29). London: Routledge.

Carrabine, E., Lee, M. & South, N. (2000). Social Wrongs and Human Rights in Late Modern Britain: Social Exclusion, Crime Control, and Prospects for a Public Criminology. *Social Justice*, 27(2), 193-211.

Carrier, N. (this issue). On Some Limits and Paradoxes of Academic Orations on Public Criminology. *Radical Criminology*, 4.

Chancer, L. & McLaughlin E. (2007). Public Criminologies: Diverse Perspectives on Academia and Policy. *Theoretical Criminology*, 11(2), 155-173.

Clear, T. (2010). Editorial Introduction to "Public Criminologies". *Criminology & Public Policy*, 9(4), 721-724.

Currie, E. (2007). Against Marginality: Arguments for a Public Criminology. *Theoretical Criminology*, 11(2), 175-190.

Garland, D. & Sparks R. (2000). Criminology, Social Theory and the Challenge of Our Times, *British Journal of Criminology*, 40(2), 189-204.

Gies, L. & Mawby, R. C. (2009). Introduction to the Special Issue on 'Communicating Criminal Justice: Public Confidence, Agency Strategies and Media Narratives'. *The Howard Journal of Criminal Justice*, 48(5), 441-445.

Loader, I. & Sparks, R. (2011a). Criminology and Democratic Politics: A Reply to Critics. *British Journal of Criminology*, 51, 734-738.

Loader, I. & Sparks, R. (2011b). *Public Criminology?* New York: Routledge.

Nelund, A. (this issue). Troubling Publics: A Feminist Analysis of Public Criminology. *Radical Criminology*, 4.

Nickel, P. M. (2010). Public Sociology and the Public Turn in the Social Sciences. *Sociology Compass*, 4(9), 694-704.

Piché, J. (forthcoming). Playing the 'Treasury Card' to Contest Prison Expansion: Lessons from a Public Criminology Campaign. *Social Justice*, 40(3).

Ruggiero, V. (2012). How Public is Public Criminology? *Crime, Media, Culture*, 8(2), 151-160.

Sanders, C. B. & Eisler L. (this issue). The Public Would Rather Watch Hockey! Promises and Institutional Challenges of 'Doing' Public Criminology Within the Academy. *Radical Criminology*, 4.

Stanko, E. A. (2007). From Academia to Policy Making: Changing Police Responses to Violence Against Women. *Theoretical Criminology*, 11(2), 209-219.

Uggen, C. & Inderbitzin, M. (2010). Public Criminologies. *Criminology & Public Policy*, 9(4), 725-749.

Woolford, A. & Hogeveen B. (this issue). Public Criminology in the Cold City: Engagement and Possibility. *Radical Criminology*, 4.

punctum books is an open-access publisher dedicated to radically creative modes of intellectual inquiry, writing, and art-practice across a whimsical para-humanities assemblage.

http://punctumbooks.com

New Release:

Jeffrey Jerome Cohen, ed., *Inhuman Nature*

Public Criminology in the Cold City: Engagement and Possibility

ANDREW WOOLFORD AND BRYAN HOGEVEEN

ABSTRACT

This paper, an exercise in autoethnography, examines how our public criminological engagement with inner city criminal justice agencies influenced our conceptualization of the "Cold City"—a term we use to describe the shifting conditions of care in urban environments whereby one is compelled to feel less responsible for the concrete (as opposed to abstract and generalized) lives of others. In particular, we explore the frustrations of public criminology, as efforts to envision justice anew and facilitate care come up against the structural limitations of the bureaucratic field in its contemporary neoliberal guise. In such circumstances, critical scholarship offers an outlet for contending with these frustrations, but also a means for imagining novel justice possibilities and revised forms of public criminological engagement.

INTRODUCTION

Critical criminology, as we have conceptualized it, is a process of opening up new spaces of possibility (Hogeveen and Woolford 2006; see also Pavlich 2001). The critical criminologist, armed with the tools of critique, sets herself against an already fabricated world of crime and crime policy bound by specific (and quite arbitrary) ontologies of harm and justice. Critique is our means to trouble these boundaries and to push toward new justice horizons not strictly beholden to the architecture of a conventional criminology that for too long has been servant to the state (Pavlich 2005).

Described here all too briefly, critique can offer the critical criminologist a feeling of the promise of potential emancipation (Hogeveen 2011). Critical criminology originates in the truth that the most marginalized are thrown into a world that is discriminatory, classist, racist, and sexist. It is not one of their choosing. Instead, powerful interests and state actors structure societal institutions (i.e. economics, education and criminal justice) to their financial, political and economic benefit, while at the same time entrenching marginalized others in tragically disadvantaged social circumstances. For instance, Canada's Indigenous peoples today experience the effects of centuries long colonization efforts by the Canadian state (Monture and Turpel 1992, Razack 2002. Despite Canada's reputation on the world stage as a humane and livable country, Indigenous peoples across this country face poverty, suicide and incarceration rates that indecently exceed those of the remainder of the country (Office of the Correctional Investigator 2002, Martel, Brassard and Jacoud 2011, Martel and Brassard 2006.

Critical criminology stands shoulder to shoulder with its radical criminology cousin in recognizing such gross injustices brought about by the capitalist and colonialist state and, more importantly, its dedication to bringing about meaningful changes that will lead to a more just, hospitable, caring and inclusive world for all—not just those who just happen to be born into affluence (Shantz 2012). It does not seek to render the criminal justice state more efficient, but takes it to task for its unwarranted buoying of the capitalist state, for its advancement of the colonialist programme, and for aggregating increasing levels of pain onto Canada's most marginalized. We are not content solely with unmasking systemic conditions of disadvantage. We are vexed by the world so often taken-for-granted and encourage other ways of being with others that push current ways of being in the world. Critical scholars grapple 'with the challenges and contradictions involved in making ameliorative changes in our social world that offer hope instead of despair, compassion instead of intolerance, and justice instead of marginalization, exclusion, and suffering' (Minaker and Hogeveen, 2009: xiii). At its core it is an art of critique that attempts to unsettle and challenge contemporary colonial and capitalist relations in the name of justice to come.

But how can one translate critique into something that is public? How might one carry this spark from the world of ideas into the world of everyday criminal justice practices? Quite often, our notion of what it means to 'do' public criminology is shaped by the expectation that the criminologist will participate in acts of public-, and most typically media-, based messaging through which the criminologist will work to shift public debates on issues of crime and punishment (see, for example, Piché 2014). However, there are other avenues for public criminological immersion and engagement, including working within and learning from those marginalized sectors of the criminal justice system—criminal justice non-profit social service agencies.

Upon beginning our academic careers, and while contributing to a collective attempt to revive critical criminology in Canada, the authors also sought to increase their social justice commitments through such direct involvement. Both had prior experiences with volunteer work in the areas of youth justice (Hogeveen) and human rights (Woolford), but in new cities, and with new professional clout, the hope was that more could be achieved.

What follows is a co-autoethnography of our experiences of public criminological involvement and its formative role in shaping our work on the "Cold City." This is a term that we use to describe the shifting conditions of care in urban environments whereby one is compelled to feel less responsible for the concrete (as opposed to abstract and generalized) lives of others. Autoethnography refers to "an approach to research and writing that seeks to describe and systematically analyze (graphy) personal experience (auto) in order to understand cultural experience (ethno)" (Ellis et al. 2011, 1). It is an appropriate methodology here because it demands that the researcher reflexively engage with his or her experiences, feelings, and emotions relating to a specific cultural and temporal context. In this manner, it is a methodology directed toward interrogating the nexus between researcher and researched, treating the assumptions and preferences of the former as constitutive components of the latter. Through the combined tools of ethnographic fieldwork and autobiographical writing, the goal of autoethnography is to open up new vistas of understanding and new possibilities for social justice. It also demands closeness to one's research and is therefore potentially resistant to the distancing effects of the neoliberalized Cold City.

We begin our paper with a description of the Cold City and then move into a discussion of how our ameliorative efforts were obfuscated by the harsh economic, social and political ethos of the contemporary non-profit criminal justice field. Despite presenting a rather dim view of straightforward confrontation of oppression in this sphere, we nevertheless remain convinced that critical public criminology is a fundamental instrument in the struggle for justice. We conclude that it proffers a point from which to imagine more just ways of being with the marginalized other who has been excluded from meaningful participation and acceptance in the world that surrounds them. It remains to the critical criminologist to conceive of more emancipatory ways of *being with* the oppressed and othered who have remained in the cold.

Being Public in the Cold City

In his examination of individuals who participate in scrounging, Thaddeus Müller (2012, 447) conceptualizes the "Warm City" as "a social environment that consists of civility, cooperation and community among strangers". The warm city is thus a space of sociability and care. In contrast, our research has focused on the Cold City, which severs this relationality, or instrumentalizes these relations as a means to advance neoliberal ends. Indeed, it is under the chill of neoliberalism that we see the Cold City tightening its icy grasp on the social service agencies that are assigned the role of providing care on our behalf. The section that follows offers a brief overview of conceptualization of the Cold City and the challenges of being 'public' in such a space (see also Hogeveen and Friedstadt 2013; Hogeveen and Woolford forthcoming; Woolford and Curran 2011 and 2013; Woolford and Nelund 2013).

With the acknowledgment that "actually-existing neoliberalism" takes specific shape as it adapts to local contexts (Brenner and Theodore 2002 and 2005; Hartmann 2005; Ong 2006), we understand neoliberalism in general as a regulatory framework for capital globalization. It is bolstered by discourses that demand that workforces become more flexible and adaptable to the needs of mobile capital, that citizens become more responsible, and that governments reduce their interference in the corporate pursuit of profit (Rose-Redwood 2006; Peck and Tickell 2007). However, alongside the "roll-back" of various social security protections, neoliberalism also entails a "roll-out" of redirected governmental controls (Chunn and Gavigan 2004; Holm 2006; Peck and Tickell 2007; Wacquant 2009b; Yesil 2006). At the local level, this "roll-out" produces a layered and complex neoliberal regulatory regime, which includes interventions such as: zero tolerance policing strategies; increased private security and surveillance; the promotion of target-hardening and risk prevention; citizen responsibilization toward entrepreneurialism and self-governance; zoning decisions and urban planning directed toward the isolation of "disordered" spaces; and, the deployment of remaining social service agencies to calculate, audit, and monitor so-called risky populations (Carroll and Shaw 2001; Glasbeek 2006; Peck 2001). Further, and to contain the fallout from neoliberal restructuring, the global prison industrial complex tends to expand under neoliberalism at exceptional rates (Wacquant 2009a).

It is in these circumstances that the conditions of care—the social circumstances that enable us to feel connection to and responsibility for others—are changing and shifting toward new strategies for controlling the poor that offer fewer opportunities for an ethic of care. In our work on the Cold City we show that it is too often the case that the help on offer in the inner city seeks to make those in need more manageable, out of view, responsible for themselves, and therefore less of a burden on our budgets and our consciences (Hogeveen and Friedstadt 2013; Hogeveen and Woolford forthcoming; Woolford and Curran 2011 and 2013; Woolford and Nelund 2013). In short, neoliberal policy and program shifts have generated a relational freeze through the imposition of compulsory managerial tasks that mediate relationships between social service providers and users in the inner city. Under these conditions, the managerial task, whether it is quantifying outcome measures, hustling to ensure economic viability, evaluating levels of risk, or establishing 'best practices', becomes the ethical focus of the modern day social service practitioner rather than the person in need (see also Brodwin 2013). And, in response, the person requesting help is required to bundle him or herself in a performance of responsibility so that they are deemed worthy of care. In other words, a person in need of help must show himself or herself to be worthy of care by embracing the language of self-improvement and responsibility that corresponds with the intended outcomes promised by specific social service agencies (Woolford and Nelund 2013).

Marginalized inner city populations are thus defined by governments, policy makers and social service agency as either "transformative risk subjects" who are to embody and accept a particular form of neoliberal self-care, or as dangerous outsiders who must be removed from social space (Hannah Moffat 2005). Our research in the Cold City has turned up many examples of how the marginalized are responsiblized by social service providers and removed from spaces of capitalist accumulation. Indigenous peoples are frequently transported from high traffic consumer space by state policing agents and/or private security. Edmonton's homeless, for example, repeatedly report being chased from shopping malls and public libraries when attempting to stave-off frostbite and otherwise find relief from the bitter cold. Others, like Jim, who seem "out of place" on account of his Indigenous heritage and homeless countenance face frequent police harassment. While sitting on a bench waiting for a bus an officer approached and questioned him for no apparent reason. The officer asked his name and when Jim refused he refused to allow him to proceed until he was more forthcoming. When he finally acquiesced the officer found that he had several outstanding warrants and arrested him on the spot. That Jim appeared out of place and thus dangerous was the officer's only justification for his intervention.

Contemporary social service agencies operate within a non-profit market in which they must compete for government and private funding. They insure continued viability by presenting outcome measures as proof to these funders that their services are in fact making a difference. Indeed, such agencies are increasingly compelled to embrace organizational practices more typical of private businesses than voluntary agencies, thereby reshaping their practices. Raising operating dollars is an ongoing and omnipotent function of the contemporary social service ethos and several agencies are hiring experts in capital accumulation. Whereas in the not so distant past such groups would be primarily concerned with acquiring those accomplished in the art of working with marginalized groups, they are now seeking those proficient in fund raising. One particular social service provider in Edmonton, for example, has an entire floor of their building dedicated to fund raising and another has hired several graduates who boast MBAs from Canada's top universities. According to Jamie this is all brought about by the contemporary competitive funding climate that he metaphorically described as a "shark tank" for its resemblance to the television program where prospective entrepreneurs compete for financial backing from wealthy funders.

The world of those who care on our behalf has always been limited by concerns beyond what will best serve those who are in need. Some would argue that a "voluntary spirit" once animated the activities of those working in the nonprofit sector before the onset of business practices (Bush 1992), but we do not agree that an era ever existed in which social service agencies did not to some degree assist the state in practices of social control (see Cohen 1985). However, the contemporary nonprofit worker finds even less time for care than was true of the welfare era, as he or she is now encouraged to emulate the entrepreneurial, managerial and competitive practices idealized in the private world of business (Baines 2004 and 2010; Evans et al. 2005; Salamaon 1993). And these emerging practices have negative implications for the ways in which care is distributed. Under neoliberalism care has become individualized. We are obligated to care for ourselves and to care for our immediate family members, but the reach of our caring does not extend much further. Moreover, under this politics of care, social service agencies, rather than care on our behalf, or through our voluntary assistance, are reconceptualized as organizations directed toward facilitating self- and family-care, so that the poor and needy, like us, can take care of themselves and their families. Lost in such a reconceptualization is an ethic of care guided by social connections beyond the family unit. Care has become immediate and narrowly local, rather than formed through mutual, open and trusting relationships with others based upon a broader shared humanity, society or environment.

To engage in public criminology in the social service field is to immerse oneself in these cold waters. In these circumstances, Amanda Nelund's (this issue) critique of the overlap between public criminology and the masculinist public sphere rings most true. The Cold City is not simply neoliberal, but also draws us toward being public in a manner that privileges the reason of the male, liberal, Euro-Canadian economic subject and subjugates the concrete experiences, needs, desires, and rationality of those who are requesting help in favour of securing scarce resources (Benhabib 1985 and 1992; Fraser 1985). Rather than propelling one into relations of care, the Cold City pushes the public criminologist towards being a frugal dispenser of care, whose ultimate aim is to make care an individual rather than relational property.

We arrived at this notion of the Cold City not simply through research and theoretical reflection, but also by engaging in public criminological work at inner-city justice agencies. Our experiences drew our attention to frigid conditions of care that characterize the contemporary Cold City.

WINNIPEG JUSTICE SERVICES:
EDs AND ORGANIZATIONAL CRISES (ANDREW)

Soon after moving to Winnipeg I was approached by two academic colleagues who recommended that I join the board of directors of a Winnipeg-based criminal justice non-profit social service agency, which I will refer to pseudonymously as Winnipeg Justice Services (WJS). They suggested it would be an opportunity for me to learn more about local criminal justice issues, and that the Winnipeg Agency was working to recreate itself as a restorative justice organization, which would fit my research interests. Although I had served as a board member for my local Amnesty International chapter, I felt absolutely unqualified, since most of my social justice engagements to this point had been of a more activist than organizational nature. Nonetheless, my colleagues were correct that it would be an education. For the first few years, I muddled through budgets and funding agreements, feeling only ever truly at home on the "issues committee," where we would discuss local criminal justice concerns and how we might improve our advocacy. Although this committee is of some relevance to the discussion of public criminology, this is not the epiphanic moment that is at the heart of my portion of this autoethnography. This moment would instead come when I found myself president of the board of directors just as a series of crises emerged.

After our longtime executive director (ED) retired, the board hired a less experienced ED to take his place. She struggled in this position for a short period before pursuing another employment opportunity. In fact, I had been president of the board for only two weeks when this ED gave me her two weeks notice. At the time, we were in an elevator on the way up to meet with the Assistant Deputy Minister of Corrections with the province of Manitoba. This obviously did not place me on very solid footing for my first meeting with our primary funder. Matters took a turn for the worse when the Assistant Deputy Minister and the Executive Director of Adult Custody asked to speak with me in private. I was seated at a table with the sun glaring directly in my eyes, as though I was under the lights for interrogation. The two large men then proceeded to threaten to withdraw all funding if they did not soon receive the sense that the province was getting "bang for its buck". Their complaint was that, as far as they could tell, the WJS had not been delivering sufficient services to their clients in correctional institutions, and they wanted to know what I was going to do about it.

Around the same time, a Federal funder contacted our office to let us know that they were auditing one of our projects because we had failed to deliver what we had promised. This was a project that had been under the direction of the previous ED and its mismanagement had been hidden from the board and her staff. Adding to the crisis, I was next contacted by the United Way, our second largest funder, and the only funder that provided us with general rather than program-specific funding, allowing us to maintain our office. They too expressed their concerns that programming was not being adequately delivered by WJS.

Under these circumstances, I felt it necessary to enlist the very language and practices I had been critically examining in my work on inner city social services. My first step was to hire an experienced retired executive director from a well-regarded social service agency to serve as our temporary ED, because the board and I did not want to once again rush our hiring process. I then assigned a competent staff member to focus on completion of the unfinished project for the federal funding for which we were to be audited. The board also initiated a hiring search through which we targeted experienced EDs. Finally, I organized a meeting with our two main funders, the province of Manitoba and the United Way, at which they were presented a five-year plan that was filled with the business-like language of the new public management: e.g., accountability, deliverables, measurable outcomes, best practices, and evidence-based programming. I learned to speak their language so that there would be no confusion about my ability to right the ship and to remake the agency into a valued "partner".

Once the crisis was averted, and our funding secured, we hired an ED with a great deal of experience, as well as a strong social justice commitment. With him at the helm, we were better able to walk in two worlds, meeting the demands of our funders while recommitting to advocacy on behalf of prisoners. But the concessions we were forced to make always seemed to be changing us, slowly reforming our practices, more than we ever changed the criminal justice system.

Although perhaps more dramatic, this is a familiar story of organizational crisis whereby agency survival eclipses all other goals. Indeed, within the neoliberal Cold City, non-profit social service providers experience a permanent state of crisis through which, at least on the surface, they are disciplined to embrace the language and logic of new public management, performing care for their 'clients' in a manner that meets the expectations of funders. In times of permanent cost-cutting and heightened funder oversight, social service providers' efforts at fostering hospitality with those who come through their doors are delimited by the extent to which these service users can be categorized, counted, and conditioned through the accountable and measureable programs of a neoliberalized social service agency.

EDMONTON JUSTICE SERVICES: GOVERNING THROUGH SILENCE (BRYAN)

In contrast to my esteemed colleague, I actively sought out participation with social service agencies shortly after touching down in Edmonton. I was convinced that as a freshly minted PhD I had much to offer and I was searching in earnest for a launching point for my critical lens. I welcomed the opportunity that serving on the board of directors for a local non-profit criminal justice social service agency, referred to pseudonymously below as Edmonton Justice Services (EJS), ostensibly provided. From the vantage point of my study of juvenile justice I was fully apprised and aware of the important work they conducted. However, my shiny optimism soon turned to gloomy cynicism.

Once on the ground and despite my earlier convictions, the demand for social justice for those marginalized by the colonialist capitalist socio-economic machine was seemingly absent. More concerned with physical and financial security, an ethic of care and commitment to unsettling the colonial condition was routinely suppressed in favour of an ethic of punishment that fixed the contemporary order. Such conventions fundamentally contribute to the very kind of quagmire social justice advocates abhor and critical scholars rally against.

Their silence and complicity made it unimaginable for me to reconcile my commitment to social justice with what I experienced. The contradictory conditions I observed were many, but allow me to offer two examples that brought my complicity with the conditions I oppose into full view. First, as part of my duties I was routinely invited to attend meetings with delegates from throughout Alberta. Gatherings were moved around the province as part of a traveling road show. When the meetings landed in their towns, local designates proudly displayed their hard work and dedication to institutional goals. On one notable occasion a van pulled up to the host hotel just as the lunch break was winding to a close. Its purpose was to take all in attendance for a tour of the local jail that would provide an opportunity for local officials to show off their hard work. Attendees were quite perplexed when I turned down the offer. Returning delegates seemed unaware of the prisoners' hardship and deprivation. They were unwilling or unable to quarrel over the gross overrepresentation of Indigenous peoples, the overcrowding, or the omnipresent systems of surveillance that characterize contemporary corrections. They left the institutional walls grateful that they were not staying behind. Once outside of the prison walls delegates were free to go about their days without having to wonder about the structural conditions that in the same instance produce their materialist prosperity and crime.

In place of critiquing present abhorrent conditions of life and proposing a just ethic of care for the most marginalized, this kind of quiet acquiescence contributes to marginalization (see Mathiesen, 2004). It became increasingly clear, however, that this organization like almost every other non-profit operating in the Cold City, could ill afford to critique or unmask the social suffering that buoys the capitalist state. This was my second insight into how social service agencies are ineffectual as platforms for and to justice. Instead of standing apart from systems of oppression, it became clear how firmly entrenched they are within them. Such a state of things was readily apparent, but became unmistakable when particularly contentious issues emerge (i.e. the proposal of particularly punitive changes in law, the treatment of prisoners and the living conditions of local houses of correction)—as they inevitably do in criminal justice circles. Instead of speaking out on behalf of the suffering other, organization officials were more or less muted lest their contrarian position raise the ire of the government on whose funding they depended for running programmes and their paychecks.

Social service agencies are locked in a precarious position: advocating too vociferously on behalf of the marginalized puts funding in peril. But this condition should not be surprising. Despite diversifying funding sources, many social service agencies in the Cold City continue to rely heavily on governmental structures to fund their essential services and to maintain their very existence. Confronted by increasingly scarce governmental funding these organizations can ill afford to critique and quarrel about the material conditions that provide the impetus for their work lest their slice of the proverbial funding pie be further eroded. Governing the other is their source of funding, their existence, and their raison d'être.

Such an ethos counters demands for, and labour in the name of, justice. Systems of marginalization and tyranny are undergirded when agencies rescind their willingness and ability to critique state disciplinary systems. Tyranny and marginalization are shored up when attention is dedicated almost entirely to garnering positive funding decisions and serving the colonialist government mandate. Gandhi was quite mindful of this dilemma. He said, "You assist an administration most effectively by obeying its orders and decrees. An evil administration never deserves such allegiance. Allegiance to it means partaking of the evil" (Ghandi 1961, 4).

Experiencing the disintegration of my desire for justice in this way was not an end. Failure in this instance suggested new beginnings and new ways of thinking about how we ought to be with others and manifested a revised ethic of care in the name of justice to come. This ethic is unbound from the guidelines and funding structures that fetter imagination. Instead it seeks out new ways of being through critique and social justice praxis. Our duty is to work toward and in the name of justice. Belief in the nobility and integrity of this principle cause is the first order.

PUBLIC CRIMINOLOGY, CRITIQUE AND POSSIBILITY

As it is commonly envisioned, public criminology seeks to mobilize research-based knowledge in an effort to shift public opinion on crime, as well as crime policy (Loader and Sparks 2011), by offering "replacement discourses" (Henry 1994, 289) that enrich and expand participatory democratic dialogue on topics of crime and punishment. These efforts might occur through "newsmaking criminology" (Barak 1988), which enlists activities such as journalism (Henry 1994), blogging (Barak 2007), public lectures (Currie 2007), service as a subject expert for the media (Henry 1994), as well as relationship building with people of influence, such as policy makers and politicians (Stanko 2007; Petersilia 2008) (for critical evaluation of all of these activities, see Piché 2014).

Presented as such, although it is intended to bring scholars out of the ivory tower, public criminology appears to be set at a distance from those who are in need of care. On the one hand, the care offered through public criminology is often a matter of opinion formation and high-level negotiation, but rarely feels immediate, direct, and situated. But on the other hand, public criminology also often immerses itself too quickly into the hegemonic public without pausing to consider the conditions of struggle that exist in this field of action. The Cold City thus presents us with a paradox when we engage the public: as we seek to get closer to the "real" world and seek to be the sponsors of change, we also become entrenched in the dominant practices and logics of the hegemonic public sphere and thereby find it challenging to play a different game.

Public criminology thus must be more than a process of translating criminological insight into the cold world of criminal justice. It cannot simply endeavor to find channels for communicating complex theoretical and empirical insights into sound bites and policy recommendations. It must rather aim to make strategic incursions into public spaces while at the same time working equally hard to counter the cooptation of critical criminology into the affirmation and reproduction of the criminal justice system (whether as privileged reformer or loyal opposition) and its criminal justice public. This requires that one also step away from the public on occasion and find spaces of critique from which one might "tirelessly question what is and what is yet to come, so as to rethink the world instead of being bound and constrained by it" Hogeveen and Woolford 2006, 692).

A danger of the positive valuation of the "public" that comes with the notion of public criminology is that we will be inclined to further disparage the "ivory tower" of academia as a space removed from engagement with the "real" world. But a tower is not simply a space of confinement. It is a place of refuge and observation that fulfills its most crucial function in times of siege. Like the "keep" in castle architecture, critique from within the walls of the university offers a space of concentric defence against the onslaught of the neoliberal ethos. It is a zone of retrenchment, a potential space of counterpublic thought (Fraser 1997), that allows one to continue to "summon logics from beyond well-established limits" (Hogeveen and Woolford 2006, 281), even while one must act within and respond to these limits. Although the university is far from a pure space, and it is certainly not untouched by the logics and practices of neoliberalism (see Sanders and Eisler this volume), it nonetheless offers interstices where critical thought can still arise and from which one can make contact with other sources of counterpublic activity, such as social movements.

We have found this space valuable in our experiences engaging within the non-profit criminal justice field, where we have felt the pull of the neoliberal ethos upon contemporary justice practices. Swept up by the everyday needs of non-profit criminal justice social service agencies, it can be difficult for one to find purchase for tactical interventions that go against the grain. Critique, then, is the refuge to which we can turn, to gather strength, strategize, reconfirm our commitments, and set our resolve against the compulsion of "there is no alternative". Increasingly, it is difficult to perform such critique from within the machinery of the bureaucratic field, and therefore marginal spaces—spaces beyond mainstream publics—are necessary seed grounds for counterhegemonic thought and practice.

In a time when criminological work is too often dismissed as irrelevant to criminal justice policy (Doyle and Moore 2011; Haggerty 2004), there is a temptation to more fully embrace the 'public' side of the public criminology equation and to become more "practical" and "relevant" in our research and public endeavours. However, the chill of the Cold City is such that it enters deep into one's bones; it offers temporary warmth in the form of small tactical victories—e.g., the provision of care to someone who has not been prescribed as worthy of care by one's programming guidelines, or a particularly pithy sound bite that perhaps stirs a moment of public debate—but is relentless in its transformation of the relations of care, making such moments more infrequent and fleeting. In such times, the scholarly, critical criminology side of public criminology is an essential resource. It is the space from which we can continue to try to imagine a possible and lasting warmth—an emancipation from the othering practices of criminal justice, or new forms of hospitality towards those in need—beyond the limited frames of responsibilizing care and disciplinary control imposed by the Cold City.

We do not, however, want to leave the impression that the space of critique is where one simply stands back from the world and indifferently dissects all that happens. Critique is a space to which one returns to try to examine and unpack the pressures of the Cold City, but it is also where we can contend with the emotions felt but suppressed amidst the need to negotiate the Cold City's demands. But the objective is always to re-engage another day and to continue the struggle to bring lasting warmth to the Cold City.

Indeed, the purpose of engaging in a critical autoethnography of our experiences in the field is to bring feeling back into the equation, to refuse the artificial separation of feeling and thought, and to find time/space in which to reflect upon the emotional and embodied aspects of our public criminological work. On a personal level, what was perhaps most frightening about public criminology within the Cold City was how it sought to drain feeling out of helping relationships—to make them business-like, responsible, and efficient. Care and concern, anger, righteous indignation, and the like were unwelcome intrusions into the day-to-day operations of non-profit social services, leaving us feeling frustrated, disappointed, and unfulfilled. These experiences are not somehow separate from the practice of critique, they are central to it, and autoethnography therefore serves as an important tool in the practice of public criminology, offering moments of self-reflection and for remembering why we are doing what we are doing.

More specifically, though, there is also a need for more engagement in public criminology from below (Ruggiero, 2010). Public criminology cannot simply occur in press galleries and halls of government; it also needs to take place through relationship formation and a politics of care that moves beyond the specifications of neoliberal managerialism. Non-profit social service agencies, caught up as they are in the politics of the Cold City, and historically operating as creatures of the state (Wacquant 2009a), also do not offer an alternate or ideal model for a public criminology from below. Instead, we seek a just ethic of care that attends to the material conditions of the suffering. Such an ethic of care would maintain, sustain and transform human beings and the society in which they live into a more hospitable space that would open out to, rather than closes down upon suffering others (Minaker and Aylsworth this volume). This kind of caring hospitality encourages social service providers to seek new ethical ways of being with the other independent of state agendas and mandates (Hogeveen and Woolford forthcoming). Derrida (2002) argues that hospitality is an 'attitude of utter openness and a readiness to give, unconditionally of all my possessions to the stranger knocking at my door' (Boersma 2004). It is this attitude of radical openness that would inspire social service agencies to unconditionally welcome and care for the other while in the same instrance challenging othering processes with much less regard for bureaucracy, accountability and state sponsored mandates.

REFERENCES

Alfred, T. 2009. *Wasase: Indigenous Pathways of Action and Freedom.* Toronto: University of Toronto Press.

Baines, D. 2004. "Pro-market, Non-market: The Dual Nature of Organizational Change in Social Services Delivery." *Critical Social Policy* 24 (1): 5-29.

--------. 2010. "Neoliberal Restructuring, Activism/Participation, and Social Unionism in the Nonprofit Social Services." *Nonprofit and Voluntary Sector Quarterly* 39 (1): 10-28.

Barak, G. 2007. "Doing Newsmaking Criminology from within the Academy." *Theoretical Criminology* 11 (2): 191-207.

Barak, G. 1988. Newsmaking Criminology: Reflections on the Media, Intellectuals, and Crime." *Justice Quarterly* 5 (4): 565-587.

Benhabib, S. 1992. *Situating the Self: Gender, Community and Postmodernism in Contemporary Ethics.* New York: Routledge.

---------. 1985. "The Utopian Dimension in Communicative Ethics." *New German Critique* 35 (Spring/Summer): 83-96.

Brenner, N. & Theodore, N. 2005. "Neoliberalism and the urban condition." *City* 9 (1): 101-7.

--------. 2002. "Cities and the geographies of "actually existing neoliberalism." N. Brenner & N. Theodore (eds.), *Spaces of Neoliberalism: Urban Restructuring in North America and Western Europe* (2-32). Malden: Blackwell.

Brodwin, P. 2013. *Everyday Ethics: Voices from the Front Line of Community Psychiatry*. Berkeley and Los Angeles, CA: University of California Press.

Bush, R. 1992. "Survival of the Nonprofit Spirit in a For-Profit World." *Nonprofit and Voluntary Sector Quarterly* 21 (4): 391-410.

Carroll, W.K. & M. Shaw. 2001. "Consolidating a Neoliberal Policy Bloc in Canada, 1976-1996." *Canadian Public Policy* 27 (2): 195-217.

Chunn, D. & S. Gavigan. 2004. "Welfare Law, Welfare Fraud: The Moral Regulation of the Never Deserving Poor." *Social and Legal Studies* 13 (2): 219-243.

Cohen, S. 1985. *Visions of Social Control: Crime, Punishment and Classification*. Cambridge: Polity.

Derrida, J. 2002. "Hostipitality." In G. Anidjar (Ed.), *Jacques Derrida: Acts of Religion* (pp.356-421). London: Routledge.

Doyle, A. & D. Moore (eds.). 2001. *Critical Criminology in Canada: New Voices, New Directions*. Vancouver: UBC Press.

Ellis, C., T. E. Adams & Arthur P. Bochner 2011. "Autoethnography: An Overview." *FQS: Forum: Qualitative Social Research Sozialforschung* 12 (1), Art. 10 – January.

Evans, B, T. Richmond, & J. Shields. 2005. "Structuring Neoliberal Governance: The Nonprofit Sector, Emerging New Modes of Control and the Marketization of Service Delivery." *Policy and Society* 24 (1): 73-97.

Fraser, N. 1997. *Justice Interruptus: Critical Reflections on the "Postsocialist Condition."* New York: Routledge.

--------. 1985. "What's Critical About Critical Theory? The Case of Habermas and Gender." *New German Critique* 35 (Spring/Summer): 97-131.

Ghandi, M. 1961. *Non-Violent Resistance*. New York: Dover.

Glasbeek, A. 2006. "'My Wife has Endured a Torrent of Abuse': Gender, Safety and Anti-Squeegee discourse in Toronto, 1998-2000." *Windsor Yearbook of Access to Justice* 24 (1): 55-75.

Haggerty, K. D. 2004. "Displaced Expertise: Three constraints on the Policy relevance of Criminological Thought." *Theoretical Criminology* 8 (2): 211-231.

Hartman, Y. 2005. "In Bed with the Enemy: Some Ideas on the Connections between Neoliberalism and the Welfare State." *Current Sociology* 53 (1): 57–73.

Henry, S. 1994. "Newsmaking Criminology as Replacement Discourse." G. Barak, ed. Media, Process, and the Social Construction of Crime—Studies in Newsmaking Criminology (287-318). New York: Garland Publishing.

Hannah-Moffat, K. 2005. "Criminogenic Needs and the Transformative Risk Subject: Hybridizations of Risk/Need in Penalty." *Punishment & Society* 7 (1): 29–51.

Hogeveen, B. 2011. 'Reconciling Specters: Promise(s) of Criminology.' In Aaron Doyle and Dawn Moore (eds.) *Critical Criminology in Canada: New Voices, New Directions*. Vancouver: UBC Press.

Hogeveen, B. & J. Freistadt. 2013. 'Hospitality and the homeless: Jacques Derrida in the Neoliberal City'. *Journal of Theoretical and Philosophical Criminology*. 5(1): 39-63.

Hogeveen, B. & A. Woolford. Forthcoming. *Cold Cities: Care and Control in Inner-City Edmonton and Winnipeg*. Under contract with McGill-Queens University Press.

--------. 2006. 'Critical Criminology and *Possibility* in Neoliberal Times.' *Canadian Journal of Criminology and Criminal Justice* 48(5): 681-703

Holm, A. 2006. "Urban Renewal and the End of Social Housing: The Roll Out of Neoliberalism in East Berlin." *Social Justice* 33 (3): 114-128.

Martel, J. R. Brassard and M. Jacoud. 2011. "When Two Worlds Collide: Aboriginal Risk Management in Canadian Corrections" , *British Journal of Criminology,* vol. 51(2), pp. 235-255.

Martel, J. and R. Brassard (2006). "Painting the Prison 'Red': Constructing and Experiencing Aboriginal Identities in Prison" . *British Journal of Social Work*, vol. 38, pp. 340-361

Mathiesen, T. 2004. *Silently Silenced: Essays on the Creation of Acquiescence in Modern Society*. New York: Waterside Press.

Minaker, J. & B. Hogeveen. 2009. *Youth, Crime and Society: Issues of Power and Justice.* Toronto: Pearson.

Monture, P. & M. Turpel. 1992. "Aboriginal Peoples and Canadian Criminal Law: Rethinking Justice." *University of British Columbia Law Review* 26: 239-279.

Müller, T. 2012. "The Empire of Scrounge Meets the Warm City: Danger, Civility, Cooperation and Community among Strangers in the Urban Public World. *Critical Criminology* 20: 447-461.

Office of the Correctional Investigator. 2012. *Spirit Matters: Aboriginal People and the Corrections and Conditional Release Act*. http://www.oci-bec.gc.ca/cnt/rpt/oth-aut/oth-aut20121022-eng.aspx

Ong, A. 2006. *Neoliberalism as Exception: Mutations in Citizenship and Sovereignty*. Durham, NC and London: Duke University Press.

Pavlich, G. 2001. "Nietzsche, critique and the promise of not being thus...." *International Journal for the Semiotics of Law* 13: 357-375.

--------. 2005. *Governing Paradoxes of Restorative Justice*. London: Glasshouse Press.

Peck, J. 2001. "Neoliberalizing States: Thin Policies/Hard Outcomes." *Progress in Human Geography* 25 (3): 445-455.

Peck, J & A. Tickel. 2007. "Conceptualizing neoliberalism, thinking Thatcherism." H. Leitner, J. Peck, and E.S. Sheppard, eds. *Contesting Neoliberalism: Urban Frontiers* (26-50). New York: Guilford

Petersilia, J. 2008. "Influencing Public Policy: An Embedded Criminologist Reflects on California Prison Reform." *Journal of Experimental Criminology* 4: 335-356.

Piché, J. 2013. "Playing the 'Treasury Card' to Contest Prison Expansion: Lessons from a Public Criminology Campaign." *Social Justice* 39 (2): 1-24.

Razack, S. (ed.). 2002. Race, Space and the Law: Unmapping a white settler society. Toronto: Between the Lines.

Rose-Redwood, R. 2006. "Governmentality, Geography and the Geo-Coded World." *Progress in Human Geography* 30 (4): 469-486.

Ruggiero, V. 2010. *Penal Abolitionism*. New York: Oxford.

Salamon, L. 1993. "The Marketization of Welfare: Changing Non-Profit and For-Profit Roles in the American Welfare State." *The Social Service Review* 67 (1): 16-39.

Simpson, L. 2011. *Dancing on our Turtle's Back: Stories of Nishnaabeg Re-Creation, Resurgence and a new Emergence*. Winnipeg: Arbeiter Ring.

Shantz, J. 2012. "Radical Criminology: A Manifesto." *Radical Criminology*. 1(1).

Stanko, E.A. 2007. "From Academia to Policy Making: Changing Police Responses to Violence Against Women." *Theoretical Criminology* 11 (2): 209-219.

Wacquant, Loïc. 2009a. *Punishing the Poor: The Neoliberal Government of Social Insecurity*. Durham, NC: Duke University Press.

--------.2009b. *Prisons of Poverty*. Minneapolis: University of Minnesota Press

Weigt, J. 2006. "Compromises to Carework: The Social Organization of Mothers' Experiences in the Low Wage Labor Market." *Social Problems* 53 (3): 332-351

Woolford, A. & A. Nelund. 2013. "The Responsibilities of the Poor: Performing Neoliberal Citizenship within the Social Service Field." *Social Service Review* 87(2): 292-318.

Woolford, A. & A. Curran. 2013. "Community Positions, Neoliberal Dispositions: Neoliberalism, Welfare, and Reflexivity within the Social Service Field." *Critical Sociology* 39 (1): 45-63.

--------. 2011."Limited Autonomy, Neoliberal Domination, and Ethical Distancing in the Social Services." *Critical Social Policy* 31(4): 583-606.

Yesil, B. 2006. "Watching Ourselves: Video Surveillance, Urban Space and Self Responsibilization." *Cultural Studies*, 20(4-5): 400-416.

The Public Would Rather Watch Hockey! The Promises and Institutional Challenges of 'Doing' Public Criminology within the Academy

CARRIE B. SANDERS[1] AND LAUREN EISLER[2&3]

ABSTRACT

With growing academic interest in public criminology there has been little beyond theorizing as to the ways in which one could actually 'do' public criminology within the academy. With this as our challenge, we implemented a departmental initiative that brought students into a for-credit course which was also open to the general public. For this paper, we utilize epistemic reflexivity to identify potential challenges and promises for public criminology that we encountered while undertaking this project. Specifically, we uncover an engaged public who are looking for ways to participate in public

---

[1] Carrie B. Sanders, PhD., Department of Criminology, Wilfrid Laurier University

[2] Lauren Eisler, PhD., Department of Criminology, Wilfrid Laurier University

[3] **Acknowledgements:** We are indebted to Justin Piché and the anonymous reviewers for their insightful critiques and suggestions throughout the review process. We are also thankful for the editorial comments and suggestions provided by Stephanie Howells and John Lortie. An earlier draft of this paper was presented at the 2013 *Critical Perspectives Conference* held at the University of Ottawa. We wish to acknowledge the financial support provided by the Noble Family, a WLU Special Initiatives Grant, VP Academic, Dean's office for the Faculty of Human and Social Sciences, and the Office of the President.

discussions concerning crime and control. We also illustrate the importance of methodology and storytelling as a tool for engaging the public. We conclude by drawing attention to the institutional and structural challenges posed against public criminology by the increasing marketization of the university.

INTRODUCTION:
IS 'PUBLIC CRIMINOLOGY' A CRIMINOLOGY FOR THE PEOPLE?

Since Michael Burawoy's 2004 presidential address to the American Sociological Association entitled *For Public Sociology*, there has been a renewed interest and growing debate regarding public intellectualism. In this address, Burawoy implored sociologists to engage "publics beyond the academy in dialogue about matters of political and moral concern" (2004, 5) and to "promote dialogue about issues that affect the fate of society, placing the values to which we adhere under a microscope" (Burawoy et al., 2004, 104). The debate has been carried over into other disciplines, such as criminology[4]. There are few topics of greater public concern than crime, criminality and crime control. Media accounts, as well as their ability to shape public sentiment of crime, can spark "moral panic" (periods of intense public fear that far outreach the harm) (Becker 1967). As a result of this emotionally charged discourse, "legislators and politicians…have replaced academics and researchers in influencing media reports and criminal justice policy" (Uggen & Inderbitzin 2010, 730; see also Garland & Sparks 2000; Zimring 1996). Public criminology, therefore, provides an avenue for academics and researchers to enter into a dialogue with various publics to attempt to shape "the ways in which crime has been apprehended and governed" (Loader & Sparks 2011, 7) and to promote the development of "sound policy and averting moral panics precipitated by extreme rare cases" (Uggen & Inderbitzen 2010, 738).

With growing academic interest in public criminology there has been little beyond theorizing as to the ways in which one could actually '*do*' public criminology within the academy.

---

[4]For the remainder of the paper we use public sociology and public criminology interchangeably.

Much of the focus has been on the development of newsmaking criminology as a means for individual academics to engage in public criminology. Newsmaking criminology refers to "the conscious efforts and activities of criminologists to interpret, influence or shape the representation of "newsworthy" items about crime and justice" (Barak 2007, 191; Barak 1994). Although newsmaking criminology has provided an important avenue for academics to participate in public criminology outside the academy, there have been no proposals or descriptions of ways in which departments or institutions, as acting bodies, can engage in public criminology (Brady 2004). As such, we executed a departmental initiative for engaging in public criminology since, as Brady (2004) states, we need a "concrete set of proposals" if public criminology is to "make a real impact" (p. 1631).

Recognizing that teaching "as a form of public criminology offers particular relevance ... because our classes often comprise future criminal justice practitioners who will be in the trenches soon..." (Uggen & Inderbitzen 2010, 740) we used teaching as a means to open a dialogue on crime and its politics. However, we expanded our publics by making a 4th year credit course *open* and *free* to the general public. Using the classroom as a means to bridge the gap between the academy and the public, we resurrected a truly "public sphere" by providing a space where academic knowledge could be brought into the public culture, and public discussion could be integrated into the academic culture (Bender 1993). As such, we attempted to legitimate and validate public criminology by making it an "integral part of our discipline" (Burawoy 2004, 9). The present paper, therefore, makes an important contribution by providing an empirical example of a departmental initiative for *doing* public criminology[5].

In this paper, we focus on this departmental initiative and explore the promises of *'doing'* public criminology within the academy. Specifically we identify an *engaged* public that is interested and looking for ways to participate in discussions con-

---

[5]We are indebted to Dr. Christopher Schneider who allowed us to model our course on his public sociology course that he designed and offered at the University of British Columbia, Okanagan campus.

cerning crime and its regulation. We also highlight the importance of methodology, emotionality and storytelling for public engagement. Further, by employing epistemic reflexivity and "dissecting the social conditions and techniques of production" (Wacquant, 2011: 441) of our engagement in public criminology, we critique the institutional shift toward 'public' engagement and intellectualism to better understand the "science-politics nexus" operating in criminology (see Wacquant 2011; Bourdieu & Wacquant 1992). From this analysis, we illuminate how institutional challenges stemming from the commercialization of the academy pose significant impediments for conducting public criminology from within the walls of the academy.

In what follows, we begin with a discussion of the present debates concerning public criminology. Next we provide a description of our 4th year colloquium series, entitled *"Crime, Deviance and the City: Public Criminologies"* and discuss the promises, such as an informed and engaged public, and challenges facing public criminology, specifically the commercialization of the academy. The challenges experienced implementing our colloquium, we argue, are illustrative of the broader critiques posed against public criminology.

PUBLIC CRIMINOLOGY: CHALLENGES OF COMMUNICATION AND INSTITUTIONALIZATION

Buroway's public sociology has been described as "advocacy on behalf of 'the public', against trends of exclusion and injustice, and for human rights and social justice" (Carrabine *et al.* 2000, 206). Public sociology builds upon C. Wright Mills' (1959, 226) conception of the sociological imagination, which required sociologists to situate human biography in history and in social structure to understand how personal troubles are connected to public issues. Mills argued that for sociology "to be of any significance, [it] must link the inner lives of people to the structures of power and ideology and the historical period in which they live" (Young 2012, 3). Without a sociological imagination, personal troubles remain that: "personal, individual and isolated pains often tinged with self-blame and doubt" (Young 2012, 4). However, "with imaginative help, the personal troubles of the many become collective issues: the personal becomes the political" (Young 2012, 4). Criminologists, therefore, employing a "criminological" imagination have been able to draw attention to harm and inequity. Burawoy differentiates public sociology, which has a "commitment to dialogue around issues raised in and by sociology," from policy, professional, and critical sociology (2004a, 8). Policy sociology, as described by Burawoy, focuses on solving questions posed by clients, or legitimating solutions that have already been identified (2004a, 9). Professional sociology "supplies true and tested methods, accumulated bodies of knowledge, orienting questions, and conceptual frameworks" (2004a, 10) and critical sociology examines the "foundation—both the explicit and the implicit, both normative and descriptive—of the research programs of professional sociology" (2004a, 10). These four 'ideal types' represent four perspectives that are internally complex but reciprocally interdependent (2004b, 1611). For example, the "core activity of public sociology—the dialogue between sociologists and their publics—is supported (or not) by professional, critical and policy moments" (2004a, 12). Yet, connections across these four ideal types, Burawoy argues, are challenged by their own cognitive practices, legitimacy, accountability, politics and pathologies (2004a; 2004b). Public sociology, Burawoy argues, loses its "moral integrity when it panders to public concerns, losing its connections to critical and professional sociology, and thus devolving into "pop" sociology" (2004b, 1611).

Criminologists working within a field of public criminology recognize their public role as "contributing to a better policy of crime and its regulation..." (Loader & Sparks 2011, 117). Loader and Sparks refer to this role as the 'democratic under-labourer' who is "to be committed…to the generation of knowledge rather than…to scoring a point or winning a policy battle…" (2010, 778). In this regard, public criminology is not solely focused on activism, but instead is concerned with generating knowledge and communicating that knowledge to multiple publics. It is about acting as a 'cooling device' and injecting rationality and civic mindfulness into debates concerning crime and its control (Wacquant 2011). Further, public criminology is concerned with evaluating and reframing cultural images of crime and criminals by designing and conducting research in conversation with communities, and disseminating that knowledge within, as well as outside, the academy (see Uggen & Inderbitzen 2010, 733-4).

Although democratic underlabouring is not necessarily concerned with activism and "winning a policy battle," for others engaging in public criminology activism is central. For those interested in activism and grassroots movements, Burawoy (2012) contends that we need more than a sociological imagination; rather we need to invoke a political imagination. For Burawoy (2012), the "political imagination depends on an organic connection between sociologists and their publics… [and] … is an essential intervention, necessary to save the university under siege from state and market…" (2012, x-xi)

Thus, much of the research conducted under the umbrella of "public criminology" aims to have "an impact on public policy and the public mind" (Currie 2007, 178) by using empirical findings to: (i) illustrate problems of public interest; (ii) draw attention to problems that may be unrecognized or ignored by the public or; iii) "engage seriously the broader impacts of social problems as well as proposed solutions, including their scientific, moral, and practical implications" (Uggen & Inderbitzen 2010, 738).

To maintain moral integrity, public criminology,

> …explicitly breaks boundaries and makes positive connections with other arenas of social action—agendas for improving services for people and communities, local and national political debates that shape policy and social provision, and crucially, with the means by which the "ordinary people", so often disillusioned and disempowered, can make claims for social justice and their human rights…[it] would be "transparent, "applied" in orientation, evidenced based, and committed to empowerment and practical (not idealistic) change (Carrarbine et al. 2000, 206-207).

Public criminology, therefore, is a call for greater academic involvement, and subsequent engagement, with issues of public concern. Not withstanding the many promises of public criminology, it has been met with resistance by some professional sociologists and criminologists who "fear public involvement will corrupt science [and] threaten the legitimacy of the discipline…" (Burawoy 2004a, 15). The purpose of the present analysis is not to discuss each critique, but instead to highlight those critiques that are relevant to the challenges met when implementing our public criminology colloquium[6]. In what follows, we look at the challenges presented by: (i) the institutional structure of academia; (ii) problems of emotionality and storytelling, and; (iii) objectivism and the science-politics nexus. We now turn to a detailed discussion on each of these critiques.

CHALLENGE 1: INSTITUTIONAL INCENTIVES AND REWARDS

Numerous scholars have argued that for academics to engage themselves in the *doing* of public criminology requires a change to the institutional culture of academia (Brady 2004; Currie 2007; Tittle 2004). Specifically, the incentive structure of the organization, which is used to make decisions regarding tenure and promotion, needs to be changed in order to recognize "public contributions" (Sprague & Laube 2009). As Brady (2004) argues, many of the scholarly pursuits academics engage in--such as publishing in high impact, mainstream journals and with 'big' university presses--are situated within a clear incentive system that impede faculty from deviating from this "unless new incentives emerge for public sociology" (p. 1632). As such, scholarship needs to be redefined if academics are to take seriously the idea of "going public". Further complicating the institutional reception of public intellectualism is an inability to both clearly define and measure public criminology. What exactly constitutes public criminology? Is it about informing public debate, or developing research with affected communities, or is it about political activism? Without a clear definition of what public criminology is and what constitutes an empirical example of public criminology the field itself cannot advance. A subsequent challenge is an inability to measure the impact of public criminology both within and outside the academy. How

---

[6]There are some very important critiques concerning Burawoy's typology and its division of labour. Feminist scholars, for example, have critiqued this 'typology' as being "overly bounded, static and nonvariable" and, as a result, unable to "adequately account for such multidisciplinary fields as social gerontology, or feminist sociology in which distinctions between professional, critical, policy, and public domains are blurred" (Creese, McLaren & Pulkingham 2009, 605). Further, Canadian scholars have correctly identified how Burawoy's description of public sociology does not consider how Canadian and American sociology differ (Davies 2009; Helmes-Hayes & McLaughlin 2009).

can one measure the success or impact researchers have to public debate?

Challenge 2: Storytelling & Emotionality

Just as the academy is not institutionally set up to reward the work of public criminologists, methodological and disciplinary training does not provide academics with the tools necessary to engage the public. As Burawoy notes, "in our attempt to defend our place in the world of science we do have an interest in monopolizing inaccessible knowledge which can lead to incomprehensible grandiosity or narrow "methodism""(2004, 17). For example, much of the research conducted within professional criminology focuses on answering a small aspect of much larger social problems and is often highly technical and quantitatively daunting, often relying on objective, cold-hard facts (see Currie 2007; Uggen & Inderbitzen 2010, 729; Young 2012). Yet, as Mopas and Moore (2012) illustrate, "taking this detached and 'objective' stance …often does very little to garner media interest and public attention" (191). For public criminologists to shape public sentiment and opinion they "must go beyond basic appeals to reason, integrating fact at the level of emotion…[and] appreciate the messiness of 'doing' public criminology" (Mopas & Moore 2012, 194-195).

Public criminology requires academics to be able to "tell good, if complex and subversive, stories which make sense to, and can be understood by, the different publics they may be addressing" (Fielzer 2009, 482). Storytelling and public engagement are challenging for a number of reasons. They require more than simply building bridges between scholars and their respective communities. They require gaining media attention, but

> …in the current political economy in which the ownership of mass media is so highly centralized, news operations are driven by profit rather than journalistic values, and political leaders are actively engaged in suppressing data and corrupting science to serve their own ideological ends, it is unlikely that much sociology will get into public discourse without the strategic coordination of the efforts of many sociologists. (Sprauge 2008, 702)

Challenges of gaining access to media have been well documented by newsmaking criminologists. Barak (1994) acknowledges these challenges and contends that newsmaking criminologists need to "build relationships" with media people, network with the organizations and participate with the newsmaking organizations that seek to influence policy. Yet, such networking requires time, patience and great energy. As a result of criminologists' inability to translate their findings and tell a story, the public, and more importantly, the media are not interested and most of what academics know "generally stays in the journals and no one ... knows about it" (Currie 2007, 180-183). Such hyperprofessionalism and insularity, some argue, has led to a self-inflicted irrelevance (Wacquant 2011).

CHALLENGE 3: RELEVANCE AND THE SCIENCE-POLITICS NEXUS

Not withstanding the importance and relevance of the challenges associated with storytelling and institutional recognition, the biggest impediment to the success of public criminology comes from the institutional and political context in which criminological research is conducted. Burawoy argues that public criminology, like critical criminology, engages reflexive knowledge, "which interrogates the value premises of society as well as our profession" (2004a, 11). He contends that in the United States it is this reflexive dimension of public and critical sociology that is in danger and not the instrumental dimension employed by professional and policy sociologies:

> Professional and policy sociologies—the one supplying careers and the other supplying funds—dictate the direction of the discipline. Critical sociology's supply of values and public sociology's supply of influence do not match the power of careers of money... This power of domination derives from the embeddedness of the discipline in a wider constellation of power and interests. In our society money and power speak louder than values and influence. (Burawoy 2004a, 18)

Canadian institutions, unlike private universities, are public institutions and as such, "public-based researchers, largely funded by public dollars feel increasingly obligated to demonstrate to the public the importance of their research and scholarly activities" (Creese, McLaren & Pulkingham 2009, 610). This has resulted in a federal government funding research that "facilitates forms of public criminology" (Creese, McLaren & Pulkingham 2009, 610). Wacquant argues, and we agree, that public criminology lacks an "objectivist analysis of the tangled circuits of production, distribution and consumption of criminological knowledge, and of the power relations that articulate them" (2011, 444). For example, how do public criminologists determine what topics of crime and crime control are 'relevant' for the public? As Rock (2010, 754) argues, "how relevance or issues of concern are defined is a matter of political contingency...one working conception of relevance has very real consequences for the discipline, and that is what the state and its agencies deem to be problematic". Politics, therefore, trump science (Rock 2010, 762). Lastly, public criminology has largely overlooked the power of the structural determinants of its production. Thus, being attentive to the "corporatization of the university" is essential for understanding the construction of criminological knowledge (Burawoy 2012, xi). As Wacquant (2011, 442) argues, before criminologists can engage in "democratic underlabouring" they need first to be reflexive and analytical about the impact of the "managerial makeover of the university...". Public criminologists, Wacquant argues, are so profoundly immersed within the institutional culture and structure that they are unable to reflect on the impact these structural conditions have on their own research and the co-construction of knowledge.

Having presented the numerous promises and challenges of public criminology, we now turn to a reflexive analysis of our departmental engagement in public criminology to uncover the promises and institutional impediments to '*doing*' public criminology within the academy.

Crime, Deviance and the City: Public Criminology Colloquium

In thinking about a way in which we could, as a department, participate in public criminology we looked at teaching as a mode of informing public conversations about crime and its control. Not unlike Burawoy (2004b, 8) we did "...not think of publics as fixed but in flux and that we can participate in their creation as well as their transformation" (Burawoy 2004, 8). As such, we used a 4th year special topics course designation created by the Department of Criminology to allow for experimentation with new courses as a space to 'create' a public by opening the classroom up to the general public.

How did we fund it?

Before we could offer the course we needed to first secure funding. Although senior administration expressed enthusiasm for the idea it quickly became apparent that there was little understanding of what the objectives of the course were and how it fit with the institutional goals expressed in the university's strategic plans. Initially we received an institutional special initiatives grant of $5000 to design the course. We approached the VP of Research for funding, but she argued that it was not "research oriented" and therefore outside the purview of her accounts. This was particularly surprising to us since knowledge translation and mobilization are key components to all research grants and projects. We then approached our Dean's Office, as well as the Office of the President who both declined funding noting they would not support a "revenue costing" speakers' series. In the end, we received funding from the VP Academics office ($2000) and the Principal of our campus ($3000) with a note stating that this was a one-time-only contribution. Shortly after securing these funds we were approached by our Development Office and told that a private donor who was a member of the community was looking to invest in a project he believed would make a significant contribution to our campus. We met with the donor to explain our vision for the course and he matched our enthusiasm and belief in the potential of the colloquium. As a result of this meeting he contributed $5000 to our project. In total we collected $15000 to cover all costs associated with the course.

How did we teach it?

The colloquium consisted of 10, three-hour classes for approximately 40 undergraduate students (for course credit) and members of the general public. Each session featured a different scholar to present their research in a publicly accessible manner to both students and members of the general public. When we chose topics of interest for the weekly presentations we tried to pick topics that would be suited to the programs offered on our interdisciplinary campus (such as Journalism and Contemporary Studies). As our campus is located on the borders of The Six Nations reserve, in a city that has, in the recent past, been identified as having a high crime rate and a socially disorganized downtown, we wanted topics that would be relevant and of interest to the surrounding community. We decided on the following topics: media constructions of female criminality; policing and crime control; cultural criminology; social media and crime; Canada's war on drugs, restorative justice; sexuality and the law; Aboriginals and the law; violence and sport; and surveillance and everyday life. After selecting the topics, we developed a list of researchers whose work we were familiar with, or whom we knew personally; if possible, we chose individuals that we had seen present in other venues. In the end, we were excited to showcase the work of Meda Chesney Lind, Peter K. Manning, Jeff Ferrell, Christopher Schneider, Andrew Hathaway, Judy Eaton, Melanie Heath, Paula du Hamel Yellowhorn, Michael Atkinson and David Lyon.

The public presentations ran for an hour and were followed by a 30-minute question-and-answer period open to students, faculty and members of the public. Following this discussion, members of the general public left and the undergraduate students, instructors and presenter used the remaining class time to engage in critical dialogue and discussion focused on the issues raised in the presentation. We constructed the colloquium in this format in the hopes of disrupting the power relations found in traditional classroom settings[7] by: (i) opening the course up to members of multiple publics and; (ii) providing a space where students and teacher could engage in meaningful and critical communication (see Freire, 2011). In this format, we not only provided an opportunity for the students to become "critical co-investigators in dialogue with the teacher", but also for the teacher, after presenting her research, to "re-consider her

---

[7]In order to avoid what Freire refers to as "banking education" whereby the teacher (i.e., the oppressor), as authority, lectures to uninformed students (i.e., the oppressed) we attempted to shift the power relations by enabling a space where both parties are "simultaneously teachers *and* students" (Freire 2011, 72).

earlier considerations as the students express their own" (Freire 2011, 81). Thus, we attempted to create a space where knowledge generation was not linear—with researcher informing public—but circular, where the public can also inform academic research.

How was it received?

The colloquium was well received and drew approximately 90 members of the public each week. The public was truly heterogeneous, including, but not limited to, active and retired police officers, police inspectors, deputy chiefs, as well as chiefs of police, students and faculty from neighbouring institutions, social service providers, judges, retired men and women, and family members of the enrolled students. The presentations were also recorded and live-streamed for others to view. Online viewership ranged from 7 to 50 viewers, with Jeff Ferrell's presentation on drift as a new contemporary crisis drawing the largest viewership. Following each presentation, participants were asked to fill out comment forms so that we, as course designers, could assess the impact and reception of the colloquium. These forms asked participants to identify whether they were enrolled in the course or were members of the general public. It also asked them how they had heard about the colloquium and then provided space for them to reflect on their general thoughts about the presentation and the colloquium. For the remainder of this paper we use these responses as well as our own experiences in designing and implementing this course as sources of data for an 'epistemic reflexive analysis' of *doing* public criminology within academe (Wacquant, 2011)[8]. Through this reflexive analysis we draw attention to the cultural and institutional elements that both shaped and impeded our public criminology colloquium, while further illustrating how our experiences are not unique but are instead symbolic of the broader structural challenges facing public criminology.

---

[8] As we continue with this colloquium we would like to conduct interviews with members of the public who have attended the lectures to acquire an in-depth understanding of how their participation in this education practice impacted and / or reoriented their understandings of the topic.

Telling Good Stories to an Uninformed Public?

As we designed the colloquium we were most concerned about identifying and inviting speakers who could easily translate their research to the general public. Being mindful of the critiques regarding academics' inability to both synthesize and communicate the importance of their research to the general public, we wondered how we could build a course that overcame this difficulty in communication. We questioned, for example, how we could provide enough background information and theoretical depth to our students and yet remain accessible to the general public. Could a public criminology course that brought together students and members of the general public, "nurture the passions students bring to justice concerns" while at the same time "narrow the yawning gap between public perceptions and the best available scientific evidence on issues of public concern" (Uggen & Inderbitzen, 2010, 726)?

A challenge, therefore, was finding the balance and finding scholars who could achieve this balance. There was the need for charismatic speakers who could be understood by a 'perceived uninformed public', as well as enhance and educate students who are familiar with the literature and field of research. The feedback from students and the general public indicate that, at least in some small way, we achieved our goal. Both students and community members reported being engaged by the issues and the format of the course. One community member provided the following feedback on the course:

> The public lectures are filling a void between the public and the university. While topics need to be appropriate and stimulating for a 4th year seminar style class, they also need to be accessible to the public –something which the public can see in everyday life. Explaining a complex theory to a member of the public that is not relevant or cannot be discussed with other members of the public doesn't bridge the gap. But if the topic was something that an attendee can discuss with his or her neighbor or colleagues, then it is accessible and will have a ripple effect in the community.

Like Fielzer (2009, 480), we found that it was important to find speakers that were able to tell good stories "through the medium of case stories and as narratives with a human interest angle". For example, the most well received lecture (by both students and the general public) was Jeff Ferrell's presentation on drift as the new contemporary crisis. Opening and closing the lecture with Woody Guthrie lyrics to, *I Ain't Got No Home*, Ferrell illustrated his theoretical arguments through the use of ethnographic examples—engaging the public on both an intellectual and emotional level (Mopas & Moore, 2012).

While we were in the processes of designing our course we heard from a variety of sources that this course would be beneficial for our students but would not succeed in attracting members of the public—as the research office exclaimed, "they would rather watch hockey". It was pointed out that people were generally uninterested in academic research findings and were content to rely on mainstream media for their sources of information on social issues. *Our experience with the course contradicts this notion and instead points to a public that is searching for ways to engage in dialogue about current social issues.* A number of members of the general public who attended the lectures stated that they wished they had access to the same materials / readings our students had prior to the presentation. They believed that access to these materials would have allowed them to be better prepared for the subject presented and to engage in dialogue with the presenter. As one community member stated, "I would have found it helpful if the public had access to suggested readings/resources on-line for further investigation either before or after the lecture." Other attendees felt that "most sessions contained enough information for you to do more research into that topic to better prepare you for the upcoming session as well as what you were able to learn from their lesson" (member of the public). This feedback challenges the notion of the uninformed and uninterested public--the public that "would rather stay home and watch hockey" (research officer). Instead it points to a public who is looking for relevant information and to engage in dialogue on social issues they feel are important. In the word of one attendee:

> I found the course gave me a renewed interest in taking more classes. Being the fact that I am over 65, the journey to get a degree does not interest me but taking subjects that interest me would be welcomed. It has awakened the drive to learn and get other views which had been gone. It has given me a purpose in life and not just to park and wait for death. Thanks. (member of the public)

That being said, our biggest impediment was drawing media interest in the series. Although our local paper ran three articles (two advertising the colloquium before it started and a third running a few weeks into the term), we were unable to get other coverage, or to even entice the local paper to meet with the presenters. Not unlike the experiences of newsmaking criminologists, we recognize that gaining access to mass communications networks requires networking—something we did not put as much attention and time towards as we should have.

The Challenges Measuring Public Engagement

Although our initial concerns focused on the need to find researchers who could "tell good stories" to an "uninformed" public, we were quickly faced with the challenge of measuring the success and impact the course would have on both the students and the general public. For example, we continually asked ourselves if we could engender change by making students and community members aware of the important social and political issues that criminologists deal with through the dissemination of academic research. We strongly believed that to affect social policy we needed to do "more than simply gain access to policy makers; we needed to engage the broader public as well…in a word, we have to educate—educate, that is, outside the classroom" (Currie 2007, 178-179). Even though we expected students to absorb and retain the knowledge presented and constructed during the lectures we did not know what type of impact the knowledge would have on the participating community members. Would they take the discussions home with them and use the information as a means of generating conversation and debate with others? Or, would the course simply act as a new form of reality crime media that the attendees would enjoy while it was running but once they left the campus they would cease to think about the issues and the implications for political and social policy? In other words, would the colloquium be reduced to a form of infotainment? As such, we were cognizant of the challenges posed against public criminology and constantly questioned if we were "simply replacing 'one symbolically-constructed reality' 'that of mass media operatives' with another, that of academics" (Ericson 1991, 220). We did not know how to overcome these challenges because we were unclear on how to measure the impact and outcome of the course. Thus, we acknowledge the challenges of measuring success; indeed there are significant challenges in defining what success actually is (see Brady 2004). If we define success as the potential to influence social and institutional change through participation in public criminology, we acknowledge that change will take time and be measured in small increments. As Diane Vaughan explained, "engaging in dialogue about issues of public concern can make change by altering the perspective of individuals or giving support to what they already think—but the full effects of such change are not always measurable or knowable" (Burawoy et al., 2004, 118). In order to determine whether or not the course was successful we considered the potential community and institutional impact.

COMMUNITY IMPACT

The public criminology course brought members of the general public to our small campus of approximately 3000 students located in southwest Ontario—some of whom had never experienced a university setting prior to their participation. One community member captured the importance of this cultural impact by stating that

> This colloquium was valuable beyond public criminology awareness. It provides a forum where community members interact with the university and helps break down the "mysteries" of higher education for those who never exposed to it. (Community member)

The course provided researchers with a unique opportunity for knowledge generation and transmission that was *cyclical* with academic knowledge translation and generation occurring from the researcher to the general public, as well as with the general public *informing* academic knowledge generation. For example, following her public lecture on regulating polygamy, Melanie Heath exclaimed, "This was an amazing experience. I have a renewed interest in my project. I was asked questions that challenged me and made me want to collect more data and ask new questions". The colloquium, therefore, challenged the traditional hierarchical structure of knowledge mobilization by providing a space for a cyclical and multi-way flow of knowledge generation with public discourse informing academic research and vice versa.

The course also provided an avenue to bring "rationality" (Kalleberg 2005) and thoughtful reason back into public discourse on crime and social control. A space that has the potential to bring "new voices to policy discussions while addressing common myths and misconceptions about crime" (Uggen & Inderbitzin 2010, 726). Although some have criticized this goal of public criminology as being "esoteric and elitist...in that experts working in academia seem to seek the help of experts working in adjacent areas and, while begging for their benevolence, try to improve the lives of others, namely non-expert actors" (Ruggiero 2010, 208), we believe that the colloquium provided a space where academic discourse and public debate could *jointly influence and shape* one another. Although we recognize the critiques posed against public criminology we strive to continually address these critiques in our future colloquiums by expanding the presenters to include academics as well as victims and advocates. Second, the colloquium may provide a cultural shift in the way we, as criminologists, view our relationship between academia and the public. By offering the colloquium within the academy we were hoping to challenge the status quo while securing legitimacy for public criminology within the academy (Mavis et al. 2012). If more public criminology courses were to develop, perhaps we would begin to see an institutional shift take place that would begin to value the work that public criminologists do– "extending peer review, testing ideas in the broader public sphere, and [thereby]... provid[ing] a career track to reward academic workers who use their positions for explicitly public purposes" (Stevens, 2008, 733).

Institutional Impact

Further, not unlike other public criminologists' experiences, our colloquium brought positive attention to our academic institution (see also Grauerholz & Baker-Speery, 2007). For example, the public criminology course successfully introduced Laurier Brantford, a campus of Wilfrid Laurier University, to students and faculty from other universities. A number of faculty members and graduate students from neighbouring universities attended sessions. Further, it drew attention to our program to prospective university students in the geographical area. This may have a positive impact on their decision of where to attend university, not only for the criminology program but for other programs at Laurier Brantford as well. In addition, the invited speakers had the opportunity to learn about the criminology program and Laurier Brantford and will take this knowledge back to their home institutions. This may have a positive impact on our MA program, in that these speakers will potentially recommend our program to their students who are considering graduate school. Also, students (both those enrolled in the course, and students who attended the course but did not receive a course credit), had the opportunity to hear from experts whose research they have read and discussed in class but would not otherwise have the opportunity to hear in person. One student summed it up by stating:

> I feel that this course was an excellent course for Laurier Brantford. It not only contributed to my learning as a student, but also invited the public and the university together [as] one. Also, personally, this course appeared to be a great fit for students in, and aspiring to attend, graduate school. It creates discussion on unconventional topics and brings a new perspective to society.

Finally, students enrolled in the course may have also benefitted by seeing how extra-academic publics interact with criminological ideas and arguments—an experience that is not only rare, but also novel within academe[9].

Acquiring Institutional Support and "Buy-in": The Science-Politics Nexus

Although our initial concerns were centred on knowledge dissemination (i.e., storytelling) and mobilization (i.e., impact) the biggest obstacle we encountered was acquiring institutional support in regards to both funding the colloquium as well as being rewarded for engaging in this "pragmatic endeavor" (Braithwaite 2005). These challenges, we argue, are symbolic of the broader science-politics nexus in which criminological knowledge is constructed.

---

[9] We are indebted to Justin Piche for identifying this potential benefit.

Institutional Shift toward Public Engagement and Knowledge Mobilization

At first we believed finding support for a public criminology colloquium would be easy as we had noticed an organizational shift towards knowledge mobilization and community partnerships. For example, much of the discourse embedded in the university mission statement fits nicely within the goals of public criminology—and more specifically, with democratic underlabouring. As the university mission statement notes: "Our commitment is to justice and sustainability…so we strive to ignite the minds, spirits and hearts of our communities through excellence in teaching and learning…".[10] This mission is carried through by the university's guiding principles. Of specific interests are the principles concerning "…community citizenship, realizing an appropriate balance among research, teaching and service, recognizing the linkage between research and teaching, [and] learning and advancing knowledge across boundaries" (http://www.wlu.ca/page.php?grp_id=28&p=188).

The importance of community partnerships and academic community engagement are further emphasized by the efforts of our research office to foster knowledge mobilization through the creation of "community profiles". These profiles provide a means for the research office to advertise the research being conducted within the institution in "accessible language" (research office, fieldnotes). The growing interest by the research office in "research stories and knowledge mobilization activities" has been established to:

> build new bridges between universities and other communities, connect university researchers with the general public, and to help broaden and deepen the public's understanding of academic research by showing its impact where they live, work and play. Having public understanding, support and pride in academic research is of the upmost importance to have academic research continue to strive and advance. (Research Office, fieldnotes)

Knowledge translation activities, therefore, are described by the university to be an essential element of the research process. In light of the University's emphasis on knowledge translation and community partnerships we were surprised when our request

---

[10] http://www.wlu.ca/page.php?grp_id=28&p=188

for funding support from the Office of the President, as well as the research office were declined on the grounds that the colloquium (an activity centred on translating research findings to the general public) was not considered a research activity.

Not unlike the university discourse supporting knowledge mobilization and community partnerships, there is also a growing trend toward knowledge mobilization and community connections from the major granting agencies in Canada (such as Natural Science and Engineering Research Council of Canada [NSERC], Social Sciences and Humanities Research Council [SSHRC], and Canadian Institutes of Health Research [CIHR]). In fact, one of the major grants offered by SSHRC—a connection grant—was established to enhance and reward knowledge mobilization activities:

> Knowledge mobilization in the social sciences and humanities facilitates the multidirectional flow of research knowledge across academia and society as a whole, in order to inform Canadian and international research, debate, decisions and actions. Those who stand to benefit from publicly funded research results in the humanities and social sciences—diverse groups of researchers, policy-makers, business leaders, community groups, educators and the media—should, ideally, have the knowledge they need, when they need it, in useful forms…The Connection program aims to support knowledge mobilization activities—such as networking, disseminating, exchanging and co-creating research-based knowledge—as an important element of publicly engaged scholarship, and as means of strengthening research agendas. (SSHRC)

The Canadian federal government, therefore, has established a grant that fosters the dissemination and exchange of knowledge. In fact, the first two (of the five) goals of this grant are to:

- Facilitate the multidirectional flow of social sciences and humanities knowledge among researchers and between the campus and the larger community, in order to enhance intellectual, cultural, social and economic influence, benefit, and impact.

- Increase the accessibility and use of social sciences and humanities research knowledge among academic and non-academic audiences. (http://www.sshrc-crsh.gc.ca/funding-financement/umbrella_programs-programme_cadre/connection-connexion-eng.aspx)

The stated goals and objectives of the connection grant are befitting of the goals of public criminology, and more specifically, of democratic underlabouring as they demonstrate a commitment to "the generation of knowledge…to be bearers and interpreters of …knowledge and to bring it to bear on matters of public concern…" (Loader & Sparks 2010, 778).

Yet, even with this growing interest in community connections and knowledge mobilization we struggled to receive institutional funding support. We wrote a SSHRC connections grant for the purpose of acquiring funding for the colloquium. When we first submitted the grant to our research office it was returned to us with editorial suggestions and some comments regarding the purpose of the project, as well as our proposed budget. It also had a note attached that identified some concerns regarding the intellectual goals of the colloquium. Specifically, the research officer noted that the media would not be interested in the presentations and the general public would "rather watch hockey". We did not know how to address the grant officer's personal criticisms regarding the intellectual merit of our initiative, but instead focused our revisions on the editorial suggestions and budgetary concerns. Once completed, we submitted the application through the granting agencies online form. A number of weeks later it came to our attention that the research officer withdrew our submitted grant. The grant manager, who withdrew our application, did not inform us of his decision, nor did he explain why it was removed. Instead, a few weeks into the colloquium, a different grant manager stated that she would like to meet with us to assist us in revising the grant. By this time, however, it was too late to reapply, as the series would be over before we could be awarded the grant[11].

This experience was not only frustrating and disheartening, but made us question the role of the grant manager and their impact on research developments. For example, are they to act as administrators, assuring that all parts of an application have been completed and the application is clear of glaring grammatical problems, or, is it their job to assess the academic merit of the research being proposed? Part of the problem, we believe, was connected back to the lack of definitional understanding of what 'public criminology' is and how the university could measure the success of this endeavor. For example, the research office did not believe this endeavor was research oriented and the office of the president felt it was a revenue costing event (even

---

[11]SSHRC funds awarded cannot be used retroactively.

though the tuition fees paid by the 35 students enrolled in the course offset a significant portion of the costs of the colloquium and the costs associated with the course were far less than the cost of running a science lab for one course in other disciplines). Nevertheless, our experiences with the research grant officers illustrate Wacquant's (2011) argument that "research administrators have more impact on what kinds of knowledge reach policy makers than the 'formative intentions' of scholars on the side of production" (444).

THE COMMERCIALIZATION OF ACADEMIA

Our experiences in regards to acquiring institutional funding and support made us question the notion of knowledge mobilization. If the central goals of the institution and of granting agencies is knowledge mobilization and community partnerships, what exactly constitutes "knowledge mobilization"? And, how do they assess the "impact" of the knowledge being mobilized? "Governments are required to make judgments about the value of research funding and, to do so, they require information on the tangible benefits or "value" provided by each program" (SSHRC 2010, 10-11). Our experiences with the research office led us to research Tri-council agencies claims regarding "knowledge mobilization" and impact assessments. From this analysis, we uncovered that the goal of funding Canadian research was not necessarily about connecting the community to the university, but instead focused on connecting researchers with partners for commercialization.

For example, the first three recommendations by the tri-council funding agencies on knowledge mobilization are to:

> Recommendation 1: Support strategic partnerships connecting researchers with business, other sectors and society at large...Effective partnerships between the academic and private sectors connect researchers and scientists with business people so that new ideas and inventions generate tangible benefits for society. We need to overcome the barriers that prevent Candaa's excellent research from being commercialized into new Canadian products, services and processes...
>
> Recommendation 2: Attract and develop talented people to meet Canada's labour market needs ...The jobs of the future will be driven by talented, skilled and creative people *who will commercialize*

innovative ideas and ensure long-term economic growth and an enviable quality of life for Canadians....

Recommendation 3: Maintain Canada's leadership position in research excellence....World-class research with global impact underpins all that the federal research granting agencies achieve for Canada...We must partner the powerful generators of new ideas with the creators of new products and services... (Tri-agency Council).

Federal government granting agencies, such as SSHRC and CIHR, "devote billions of dollars every year to research and are responsible for showing that publicly supported research and related activities lead to tangible short—and long-term benefits" (SSHRC 2010b, 1). As such, commercialization and 'tangible' outputs appear to supersede community partnerships and engaged discussions concerning crime and its control. As long as research impact is measured in 'tangible' ways public criminology initiatives are challenged.

Further, allowing criminologists to report their research findings, which often go against everyday understandings of crime and its control, places the university—and more importantly, its ability to establish strong working relations with industry and political figures—in a tenuous position. In fact, the importance of maintaining positive relations with the public was something that we were consciously aware of during the design of the course. For example, we selected topics that were 'hot topics' as they were prevalent in the news, and we believed would be both relevant and of interest to the public. We were also cognizant to not be too risqué in our choices because our future funding would rest on the success and reception of our first colloquium. Through this experience, we recognized that defining relevance was a political matter that can "lead people to choose sides and through commitments, fears, and concerns can lead to censorship of topics" (Rock 2010, 762). As such, notions of relevance can have significant consequences not only for academics and their ability to acquire funding and conduct research, but also for the public who can remain uninformed about topics that may cause greater harm than those that are perceived as more relevant (Rock 2010, 762). Thus, our own concerns regarding attracting and sustaining public interest while maintaining institutional support and buy-in for the colloquium draws important attention to the ways in which societal and institutional structures shape criminological engagement more generally.

For public criminology to succeed and receive institutional support we believe that knowledge mobilization and impact must be redefined. If academic institutions and granting agencies are truly interested in knowledge mobilization then understandings regarding knowledge translation need to be expanded and appreciated.

> Translation of knowledge gained has to be integrated into the research plan, not merely an add-on. If societal impact is truly a desirable goal, then all funders of research need to take seriously how challenging, difficult and time consuming it is to actually engage with stakeholders to make research knowledge more community oriented (SSHRC 2010b, 8).

The institutional challenges that we faced in implementing this colloquium, stemming from the commercialization of the academy, therefore, are illustrative of broader critiques posed against the notion of democratic underlabouring and the broader idea of public criminology (see Wacquant, 2011).

Discussion and Concluding Thoughts

With growing interest in public criminology it is imperative that we move beyond merely theorizing to instead exploring ways to breakdown the institutional and structural challenges posed against public criminology. Although newsmaking criminology provides guidance for criminologists to participate "... in the newsmaking process as credible spokespersons, ... [and] to redefine the parameters of acceptable or favorable themes about crime and justice" (Barak 1994, 250), there has been little guidance for departments to participate in public criminology (Brady 2004). We have attempted to address this gap in the literature by outlining our own departmental initiative as a resource for future reference and adoption.

Reflecting on our own experiences doing public criminology from inside the academy we identify a number of promises and rewards. For example, our colloquium provided a means for us to live out the mission of our university by advancing knowledge across boundaries and to deepen and broaden public understanding of academic research by showing its impact where they work, live and play. The colloquium, we argue, created a truly "public sphere"—a space many have argued has dissipated - and enabled new voices to be brought to policy debates (Bender 1997). It also provided evidence against the notion of an uninformed and uninterested public and brought a renewed interest and respect to academic's work in the public arena. Our reflexive analysis highlights the importance of storytelling for public criminology. Our experience, in watching the public's reception of criminological research, reaffirms feminist critiques concerning the importance of methodology and emotionality in public criminology. The presentations that moved beyond a narrow methodological discussion focused solely on 'objective' statistical facts and instead incorporated case studies and ethnographic data engaged the community on both an intellectual and emotional level and were by far the best received (Mopas & Moore 2012).

Further, we believe that our engagement not only enhanced the reputation of our academic institution, but may have also provided personal and professional rewards for the individual presenters (for similar arguments see Grauerholz and Baker-Sperry, 2012). For example, we faced a number of challenges acquiring institutional support when designing the colloquium. This lack of support, we argue, was connected to the varying definitions and understandings regarding public criminology. However, following the end of our first colloquium we received recognition for the success of the series as well as financial support from the Dean and the office of the President to offer the colloquium again[12]. Such benefits, we contend, may lead to a cultural and institutional shift fostering a new type of respect and recognition of public engagement. Thus, by promoting public criminology from within the academy we have attempted to legitimize and validate the practice.

Although our colloquium uncovered a number of promises for public criminology, it also illuminated important institutional and structural challenges facing public criminology. Our desire to have 'relevant topics' that would be of interest to our publics and garner *positive* attention for the series, as well as

---

[12]Presently the Dean is working to establish permanent funding for this colloquium.

for our department and institution, illuminates the political nature inherent in public criminology. As Burawoy cautions, "public sociology, no less than policy sociology, can be held hostage to outside forces. In pursuit of popularity public sociology is tempted to pander to and flatter its publics, and thereby compromising professional and critical commitments" (2004 17). As such, we cannot ignore the intensely political environment in which criminological knowledge is constructed (Rock 2010, 764).

Additionally, by analyzing our challenges in acquiring institutional support we were able to locate our struggles within the broader structural changes occurring across Canadian universities. Specifically, we have illustrated how the increasingly managerial makeover of the university shapes the work that occurs within it. For example, by examining the institutional and Canadian federal government granting bodies' shift toward community engagement through knowledge mobilization and translation initiatives, we have uncovered the ways in which commercialization supersedes community partnerships. Our experiences have also reinforced the need to redefine our understanding of impact. As long as impact is measured in 'tangible' ways, public criminology initiatives will remain challenged. Further, knowledge mobilization and translation needs to be redefined to acknowledge the importance of methodology and storytelling in order to support pubic engagement. We believe our public criminology colloquium, which brought together members of the public, students, and faculty in partnership to examine and discuss a wide variety of important social issues represents one small positive step in this redefining process and in the development of a truly public criminology.

BIBLIOGRAPHY

Barak, Gregg. 2007. "Doing newsmaking criminology from within the academy" *Theoretical Criminology* 11: 191-207.

Barak, Gregg. 1994. *Media, Process, and the social construction of crime: Studies in newsmaking criminology*. New York: Garland Publishing.

Becker, Howard S. 1967. "Whose side are we on?" *Social Problems* 14: 239-247.

Becker, Howard S. 2003. "Making Society Relevant to Society." Paper presented at the meeting of *The European Sociological Association* Murcia, Spain.

Becker, Howard S. 1995. "The power of inertia" *Qualitative Sociology* 8: 30-309.

Bender, Thomas 1997. *Intellect and Public Life*. Baltimore: The Johns Hopkins University Press.

Bourdieu, P. and Wacquant, L. 1992. *An Invitation to Reflexive Sociology*. Chicago: University of Chicago Press.

Brady, David. 2004. "Why Public Sociology May Fail" *Social Forces* 82 (4): 1629-1638.

Braithwaite, John 2005. "For public social science" *The British Journal of Sociology* 56 (3): 345-393.

Burawoy, Michael 2012. "Forward" pp. x-xi in Nyden, Philip, Hossfeld, Leslie, and Nyden, Gwendoly ed. *Public Sociology: Research, Action, and Change*. London: Sage publication.

Burawoy, Michael 2004a. "For Public Sociology" *American Sociological Review* 70 (1): 4-28.

Burawoy, Michael 2004b. "Public Sociologies: Contradictions, Dilemmas, and Possibilities" *Social Forces* 82 (4): 1603-1618.

Burawoy, Michael, Gamson, William, Ryan, Charlotte, Pfohl, Stephen, Vaughan, Diane, Derber, Charles and Schor, Juliet. 2004. "Public sociologies: A symposium from Boston College". *Social Problems* 51: 103-130.

Carrabine, L. Lee, Maggy, South, Nigel. 2000. "Social Wrongs and Human Rights in Late Modern Britain: Social Exclusion, Crime Control, and Prospects for a Public Criminology." *Social Justice* Vol. 27, No. 2

Chancer, L. and McLaughlin, E. 2007. "Public Criminologies: Diverse perspectives on academia and policy". *Theoretical Criminology* 11: 155-173.

Creese, G., McLaren A. T., Pulkingham, J. 2009. "Rethinking Burawoy: Reflections from Canadian". *Canadian Journal of Sociology* 34 (3): 601-622.

Currie, Elliott. 2007. "Against Marginality: Arguments for a public criminology" *Theoretical Criminology* 11 (2): 175-190.

Davies, S. 2009. "Drifting Apart? The institutional dynamics awaiting public sociology in Canada" *Canadian Journal of Sociology* 34 (3):623 – 654.

Ericson, R.V. 1991. "Mass media, crime, law, and justice" *British Journal of Criminology* 31: 219–49.

Feilzer, Martina. 2009. "The Importance of Telling a Good Story: An Experiment in Public Criminology" *The Howard Journal* 48 (5): 472-484

Freire, Paulo. 2011. *Pedagogy of the oppressed.* New York: Continuum.

Garland, D. 2001. *The Culture of Control.* IL: The University of Chicago Press.

Garland, D. and Sparks, R 2000. "Criminology, Social Theory and the Challenge of Our Times" *British Journal of Criminology* 40(2): 189-204.

Grauerholz, Liz and Baker-Sperry, Lori 2007. "Feminist research in the pubic domain: risks and recommendations" *Gender & Society* 21(2): 272 – 294.

Helmes-Hayes, R and McLaughlin, N. 2009. "Public Sociology in Canada: Debates, Research and Historical Context" *Canadian Journal of Sociology*, 34(3): 573 – 600.

Kalleberg, Ragnvald 2005. "What is 'public sociology'? Why and how should it be made stronger?" *The British Journal of Sociology* 56 (3): 387-393.

Loader, Ian and Sparks, Richard 2010. "What is to be done with public criminology? *Criminology and Public Policy* 9(4): 771-781.

Loader, I. and Sparks, R. 2010. *Public Criminology?* London: Routledge.

Mavis, M., Dolgon C., Maher, T and Pennell, J. 2012. "Civic Engagement and Public Sociology: Two "Movements" in Search of a Mission" *Journal of Applied Social Science.* 6:5: 5-30.

Mopas, Michael and Moore, Dawn. 2012. "Talking Heads and Bleeding Hearts: Newsmaking, Emotion, and Public Criminology in the Wake of a Sexual Assault". *Critical Criminology* 20: 183-196.

Nielsen, Francois. 2004. "The Vacant "we": Remarks on Public Sociology" *Social Forces* 82(4): 1619-1627.

Rock, Paul. 2010. "Comment on "Public Criminologies" *Criminology and Public Policy* 9(4): 751-767.

Ruggiero, Vincenzo. 2012. "How public is public criminology?" *Crime Media Culture* 8(2): 151-160.

Ruggiero, Vincenzo. 2010. *Penal Abolition.* New York: Oxford University Press.

Schneider, Christopher. 2011. *Public Sociology Course Outline.* University of British Columbia: BC:.

Sprague, Joey and Lauge, Heather. 2009. "Institutional Barriers to Doing Public Sociology: Experiences of Feminists in the Academy" *American Sociology* 40: 249-271.

Stevens, Sharon M. 2008. "Speaking Out: Toward an Institutional Agenda for Refashioning STS Scholars as Public Intellectuals." *Science, Technology, & Human Values*, 33 (6): 730-753.

Tittle, Charles. 2004. "The Arrogance of Public Sociology" *Social Forces* 82 (4): 1639-1643.

Tri-agency Council. *Creating Canada's Future: Investing in Research for Impact Today and Tomorrow.* Canadian Institutes of Health Research,

Natural Sciences and Engineering and Social Sciences and Humanities Research Council of Canada Report.

Uggen, Christopher and Inderbitzin, Michelle 2010. "Public Criminologies" *American Society of Criminology* 9(4): 725-749.

Wacquant, Loic 2011. "From 'Public Criminology' to the reflexive sociology of criminological production and consumption: A Review of Public Criminology?" *British Journal of Criminology* 51: 438-448.

Young, Jock. 2011. *The Criminological Imagination*. Cambridge: Polity Press.

Zimring, F. 1996. "Populism, Democratic Government and the Decline of Expert Authority: Some Reflections of "Three Strikes" in California", *Pacific Law Journal* 28 (1): 243-56.

Troubling Publics: A Feminist Analysis of Public Criminology

AMANDA NELUND

ABSTRACT

Public criminology has emerged as a type of criminology committed to making change. This is a sentiment strongly shared by feminist criminology. There is nothing in the public criminology literature, however, that would guarantee that the type of change made would be transformative or critical. A feminist analysis of public criminology reveals an erasure of power relations in the production of knowledge, the concept of the public, and the reception of knowledge claims. This paper argues that it is only by addressing these feminist critiques and paying attention to power that we can build a transformative public criminology.

INTRODUCTION

The idea of public criminology, of engaging the public with criminologists' work and making practical change, has generated a lively discussion amongst academics. Yet the voice of feminist criminologists has, thus far, been relatively silent on the subject. This is simultaneously surprising and understandable. While feminist criminology has a rich history of engaging different publics, its work does not take on or conform exactly to public criminology as so far conceptualized. A feminist analysis of the concept of public criminology reveals a troubling lack of attention to power and power relations. Feminism can contribute to the public criminology conversation by highlighting the role of power and, in so doing, assist in the practice of a critical public criminology.

This paper begins with an outline of the public criminology literature. I argue that this literature shares with feminism a commitment to change making. Despite this affinity there is no guarantee that the type of change addressed in the public criminology literature will be satisfying to feminist criminologists. I look at the erasure of power relations in the epistemological assumptions of public criminology, the ways in which it conceptualizes the public and our relationship as academics to that public, and in the ways that our work as feminists is received. Throughout the paper I argue that one alternative way to think about the same types of issues raised by public criminology, one that may serve us better as critical scholars, is Patricia Hill Collins' concept of intellectual activism.

Public criminology is a relatively new term that grapples with an old issue. How do we use academic research outside of the academy? Supporters of public criminology argue that academics should hold an active and engaged role in making social change. Currie (2007) describes public criminology as a criminology that "takes as part of its defining mission a more vigorous, systematic and effective intervention in the world of social policy and social action" (176). A key goal of this approach is to impact both public policy and the public mind (Uggen & Inderbitzin, 2010). This can be done in a variety of ways but a commonly discussed strategy is the dissemination of criminological knowledge through mass media engagement (Uggen & Inderbitzin, 2010; Currie, 2007; Feilzer, 2009). A closely related concept, then, is Barak's notion of newsmaking criminology. Newsmaking criminology strives, similarly to public criminology, "to affect public attitudes, thoughts and discourses about crime and justice" (Barak, 2007: 192). The overall spirit of this literature is to engage with and change public ideas and around and responses to crime (Loader & Sparks, 2011).

Feminist approaches to criminology are similar to public criminology in regards to this focus on change making. Feminism is a large and diverse perspective, but it is the coupling of the recognition of and a commitment to the ending of the oppression of women in society that unifies the many disparate positions (McLaren, 2002). Feminism involves theory about oppression and strategies for change (Daly & Chesney-Lind, 1988). Risman (2006) argues that feminist sociology has always been public "if by 'public sociology' we mean sociology engaged with an audience outside the academy, with an intent to create and use knowledge for the public good" (281). Creese, McLaren and Pulkingham (2009) point out that academic feminists in Canada have been and continue to be in contact with activist feminists, government officials and members of other publics. This is, of course, not only a feminist ideal. Engaging with different publics has also been essential to the work of Indigenous, postcolonial, queer and other critical perspectives. Feminist approaches to criminology thus share with public criminology a spirit of engaging and influencing the public.

Feminism reminds us of the centrality of making change and also stands as a particularly vivid example of doing that type of work. We have a rich history of this in Canada, both from the feminist movement generally and from feminist criminology in particular. Feminist criminologists have worked, in a variety of capacities, to bring attention to various forms of victimization, including intimate partner violence and sexual assault (Comack 2006; Doe, 2003; Levan 1996; Gotell, 2012). They have been integral in facilitating changes to prisons for women and our understanding and treatment of criminalized women (Comack 1996; see Hannah-Moffat & Shaw 2000; Hayman 2006). Feminist criminologists have changed laws, worked with governments, brought violence against women into the public spotlight and mobilized with feminist organizations, such as Women's Legal Education and Action Fund and Canadian Association of Elizabeth Fry Societies, across the country to make change occur on the ground.

Feminist criminology, in the main, is focused on making a particular type of change. The focus is on ameliorating the oppressive discourses and social conditions of patriarchy, capitalism, colonialism and other structures. That is to say, it shares with other strands of critical criminology a focus on transformative change. The goal is not to contribute to the better management of "criminal" populations or evaluate criminal justice policy better, but to critique criminal and social justice realities and attempt to push the bounds of possibility and thought (Hogeveen & Woolford, 2006). Although similarly focused on making change, there is nothing inherent in the idea of public criminology that would ensure critical or radical change making. For example, James Q. Wilson, author and advocate of Broken Windows theory, and Ronald Clarke and Marcus Felson, authors of Routine Activities Theory, are identified as successful public criminologists (Tonry, 2010). These individuals have used their scholarship, theory and empirical work, to change policy and inform the public. They have successfully inserted their ideas in to the public realm and helped shape public perception of what crime is and what the response to crime should be. The criteria for being a public criminologist includes engaging the public, it does not include a commitment to doing so from a critical perspective. In order to be acceptable for those working from a feminist or other critical standpoint public criminology must be committed to making not only to social change but to social justice. Snider reminds us that making change is not difficult, but rather that the difficult task is "making change that matters to disempowered, marginalized people, change that provides tools they can use to lessen oppression, challenge repressions, and change the relations of power" (2006: 323). Feminism alerts us to the importance of power relations in how we think about and practice public criminology and how it is received. In this way it can both help identify some of the limits of the current public criminology conversation and offer some ideas for practicing a critical approach to change.

Public criminology is defined differently by different authors but a general tendency in this literature, as Sparks and Loader (2010) point out, is to import Michael Burawoy's (2005) schema of types of sociology and sociologists. He identified four types of sociology: professional, critical, policy and public. Professional sociology is at the centre of the discipline; it provides the methods, research questions, and major findings and theories of sociology. Critical sociology interrogates the foundations of professional sociology. Both of these are directed towards an academic audience. Public and policy sociology are done for extra academic audiences; policy sociology is done at the behest of a specific client while public sociology is done in order to create a conversation with the public (Burawoy, 2005). Uggen and Inderbitzin (2010) utilize this schema and describe public criminology as helping to "evaluate and reframe cultural images of crime, criminals and justice by conducting research in dialogue with communities and in disseminating knowledge about crime and punishment" (733). Although they note the research role of the public criminologists, the most highlighted task of pubic criminology is translation and dissemination of professional criminological scholarship. Though some who use Burawoy's schema, such as Uggen and Inderbitzen (2010), recognize the limits of such rigid distinctions, they continue to bring Burawoy's work into the public criminology conversation. Newsmaking criminology outlines a slightly different role for criminologists; while the goal is still to bring knowledge to the public, Barak calls upon her to take a side (Barak, 2007). The newsmaking criminologist should "interpret, influence or shape the representation of 'newsworthy' items about crime and justice" (Barak, 2007: 191-2). This conceptualization of public criminology, particularly the use of Burawoy's schema but also Barak's identification of a discrete type of criminology that is newsmaking, limits the transformative potential of this type of work. Feminist theory contains a number of concepts that could enable the more critical practice of public criminology.

PUBLIC CRIMINOLOGY AND INTELLECTUAL ACTIVISM

An alternative way of thinking about change making, one that addresses power relations, is Patricia Hill Collins concept of intellectual activism. Collins describes intellectual activism as "the myriad ways that people place the power of their ideas in service to social justice" (2013, ix). From the beginning this is an approach which is committed not only to social change of any type as public criminology is, but to social justice and transformative change. Although Collins notes that the mechanisms with which to do this are broad, ranging from creating poetry and other arts based mechanisms, to writing social theory, to practicing critical teaching. She argues that "because ideas and politics are everywhere, the potential for intellectual activism is also possible everywhere" (Collins, 2013, xii). This allows for opportunities for making change through scholarship, be it theoretical, policy oriented, critical or clearly public. It does not hierarchize these types of work or any aspect of the academic endeavour, be it teaching, service, or research. Collins (2013) also provides two broad strategies for engaging in this work: Speaking truth to power, in which we challenge the foundations of existing power relations; and Speaking truth to the people, or bringing our ideas to people who are unlikely to be exposed to them. Whether speaking truth to power or to people Collins argues scholars must be attuned to their own social positioning and how it affects the scholarship they produce. It is important to incorporate an intersectional analysis, one that looks beyond the author's own identity to account for intersecting structures of oppression. Failure to do so can result in the erasure of some groups' experience and the construction of policy that neglects or harms some groups of people, as Crenshaw illustrates with the example of violence against women of colour (Crenshaw, 1991). When entering into a conversation with different publics it is crucial that academics be attentive to different identities and social positions.

Public criminology, both as a label and as a literature, sets up a binary: academic work is either public (or newsmaking criminology) or some other version of criminology. This binary is not simply describing two different types of work; instead it is similar to the private/public dichotomy in that it "is best understood as a discursive phenomenon that, once established, can be used to characterize, categorize, organize, and contrast virtually any kind of social fact: spaces, institutions, bodies, groups" (Gal 2004, 264). Naming it public criminology is a discursive move, used to categorize and contrast different types of knowledge and knowledge work. If public criminology is engaged, political, pragmatic and accessible then other criminologies are detached, objective, and aloof. Not only does this set up a binary, it creates a hierarchy based on traditional markers of scientific thought that excludes alternative ways of producing knowledge.

The use of this binary rests on a problematic epistemological assumption that ignores the power inherent in the production of knowledge. It assumes the possibility that you can have detached, objective, non-political knowledge. This is an assumption that underlies much public criminology work. Turner (2013) identifies this position as "fighting for truth" and outlines the positivistic assumptions underlying it, arguing that the "normative ideal implied in the 'fighting for truth' perspective on criminology's public role is that criminology can, and should, be an objective, scientific pursuit that provides conclusive 'truth' about crime and criminality" (152). This is a position that has been consistently critiqued by feminist theorists. Creese, McLaren and Pulkingham (2009) argue that feminism has always been shaped by the fundamental assumption that because all knowledge is socially situated, all knowledge is political. Standpoint feminism has long argued that the identity of the producer of knowledge matters (Smith, 1987; 1990). The idea that we can have scholarship that has no political allegiance and comes from no particular position has been critiqued for substituting an idealized liberal and largely masculinist or androcentric perspective, in lieu of material and situated perspectives. In this sense, because it is seen as general and nonspecific it is a view from nowhere (Haraway 1988). Alternatively, feminists have long struggled to identify their research as offering a situated knowledge, and thus one that is partial and subjective. This reification of objective knowledge is both inherent in the binary but also stated outright by many advocating for public criminology. Rock (2010), for example, argues that the criminologist should be "the disinterested observer" (757) who simply seeks to understand, not take sides.

Often the practice of public criminology, particularly when engaging with media, pushes us to present our knowledge as objective. Rather than encourage the presentation of partial and situated knowledge, "public interlocutors–be they lawyers, journalists, politicians, or citizens–demand that sociologists tell them the truth, the whole truth and nothing but the truth" (Stacey 2004, 138). In order to be a credible expert one must present her or his knowledge as *the* truth. Uggen and Inderbitzin (2010) argue that "it becomes the responsibility of public criminologists to translate their findings and their science into terms that the public and the press can interpret and understand easily" (729). Science, in the public realm and in much of the public criminology literature, is understood to be positivist and objective (Stacey 2004), meaning that scholars risk feeding this misperception through participation in traditional forms of public criminology.

Collins's work on black feminist thought and epistemology remain at the heart of her intellectual activism. Collins outlines the contrasting epistemological standards between positivist and black feminist approaches: distance between the knowing subject and known object, the absence of emotion, removal of ethics and values from the research process and adversarial debate versus lived experience as a way of knowing, an ethic of care, personal accountability, and dialogue (Collins, 2000). The overarching difference between the two perspectives is the attention paid to social position and power. This is not to say that in order to engage in intellectual activism one must be working from a black feminist standpoint, instead "the significance of a Black feminist epistemology may lie in its ability to enrich our understanding of how subordinate groups create knowledge that fosters both their empowerment and social justice" (Collins, 2000: 269). By setting up academic work as objective the public criminology literature denies these different standpoints and legitimates only dominant and potentially normative standpoints, epistemologies and truths. Not only has Collins spent years developing a black feminist standpoint but she insists that all intellectuals think through their positioning, how it affects their intellectual work and how it affects the truths that they create. Paying heed to this epistemological critique can assist us in ensuring our work does not reproduce dominant and oppressive relationships or positions. Public criminologists must pay attention to where they are situated and must also pay heed to whom they are trying to address.

Who or What is "The Public"?

One of the weakest aspects of the public criminology literature is its cursory conceptualization of who or what constitutes "the public". In many cases the idea of the public is left entirely undefined (Barak, 2007; Loader & Sparks, 2010, 2011; Uggen & Inderbitzin, 2010). In some cases quotations are used when talking about "the public," suggesting that this is not a self-evident concept, but no elaboration is given (Carrabin, Lee & South, 2000; Feilzer, 2009). Currie (2007) alludes to a definition when listing those with whom researchers should engage. His public includes "policy makers, journalists, the general public, community leader and non profit organizations" (Currie,

2007: 187). Kramer (2009) uses Burawoy's work to define the public as "people who are themselves involved in a conversation" (Burawoy 2007: 28). Throughout the public criminology "the public" is presented as needing no or very little definitional work.

This is a serious limitation of public criminology when it comes to its ability to foster transformative change. The public is sometimes referred to as a space, "the public arena" (Currie, 2007) or "the public sphere" (Barak, 2007), which feminist theorists have shown to be exclusive in nature. Historically the public sphere is a masculine one, where men and their activities reside in contrast to the feminine private sphere (Benhabib 1992; Fraser 1989). Similarly, Fraser (1989) argues the role of citizen is an inherently masculine role. In Canada we must also consider the classed and racialized nature of citizenship, where the western citizen is white and middle class (Razack 2002). Because citizenship is conceptualized in this way, the public sphere and the conversation there is based on norms and meanings that are particular to that citizen and their situated and privileged experiences (Fraser 1989). Thus when scholars enter the public sphere and engage in dialogue with citizens they run the real risk of only engaging with those people who have been marked as citizens and of bolstering a privileged subject position at the direct expense of marginalized others.

The boundaries of the public sphere are not natural or obvious; rather, they are discursively and materially built (Fraser 1989). Where do public criminologists place the boundaries around public space and what types of work do those boundaries allow for? In order to address the large traditional public sphere, public criminology would be limited to newsmaking criminology or other forms that ensure our work would be accessible to the broader public sphere. In retaining the traditional boundaries to their work, scholars reinforce those boundaries. Feminist scholars have also pointed to the malleability of the boundaries between public and private (Gal 2004). Feminist criminologists in particular have worked tirelessly to redraw those boundaries so that intimate partner violence, sexual assault and sexuality are pulled into the public sphere. If scholars retain the traditional borders they risk losing sight of a host of activities, injustices and crimes. Yet it may not be enough to simply redraw the boundaries as Fraser (1989) argues, in order to achieve emancipatory social outcomes we must transform "the content, character, boundaries and relations of the spheres of life" (137). Feminist work has shown the difficulty in achieving justice for gendered violence in a public sphere which maintains traditional ideas about sexuality and still sees the reasonable person as male (Naffine 1987; Smart 1995). This illustrates the problem of redrawing the boundaries without fundamentally changing the content of the public and private. Critical scholars should not be content to enter the public sphere without challenging its make up and assumptions.

In the public criminology literature the public is most often considered a group. We are bringing our work "back to the people" (Carrabine, Lee & South, 2000) by explaining our work to the public (Uggen & Inderbitzin, 2010). Even before critically examining the idea of the general public, this conception is limiting for scholars. If the entire Canadian population makes up the public we cannot possibly engage interactively with them, we must simply transmit knowledge in the most uniform manner possible. If we use the idea of the general public we are limited to forms of engagement wherein the general public is a passive recipient of our expert knowledge.

As I have already argued, not every Canadian citizen constitutes the group known as the public. There is an assumption here that Canadian society has one, democratic public that we all participate in equally. Feminist scholars have consistently found that to be false. Instead the public has been made up of primarily economically and racially privileged men (Fraser 1990). If, as critical scholars, we wish to challenge social inequality rather than reinforce it we would be better served to work with counterpublics. Fraser (1990) argues that throughout history there is evidence of oppressed groups coming together to form subaltern counterpublics, which are "parallel discursive arenas where members of subordinated social groups invent and circulate counter discourses, which in turn permit them to formulate oppositional interpretations of their identities, interests, and needs" (67). As critical scholars committed to social justice these are publics with which we should be engaging. When we do so our strategies for engagement must become more interactive as we work with counterpublics and bring their knowledge into our criminological work. This is not to exclude work with more traditional publics but to point to how counterpublic groups are hidden and silenced when "the public" remains undefined.

There are a number of assumptions about the position of the academic in relation to the public. For example, there is an assumption that academics do not already belong to an identifiable public, that they did not come to the academy as a way to serve that public, or that they do not take their work to their public on a daily basis. When discussing public sociology scholars of colour and working class academics described their connection to their communities as a given (Sprague & Laube 2009). This connection was not something they chose to establish; instead it was a constant in their academic life. The assumption that we can choose to engage with different publics and do not have established ties problematically reinforces the idea of a view and the academic from nowhere.

A related but different assumption is that the privilege accorded to academics will be enough to overcome markers of marginalization, allowing us sufficient credibility to "the public." Or that the positioning of the academic will allow them to engage with any public they choose. Can I engage with any public and be a credible expert? As a young woman and academic my entry in to the general public is marked in ways that typically do not lend themselves to denoting expert status. However, am I seen as more credible than the actual groups with which I am working? There is a risk that those of us who are working with marginalized groups of which we are not a part begin to speak for those groups. Our privilege will mean that we are taken more seriously and our voices will be the ones invited to speak to the media or in other public forums while the voices of the marginalized continue to be silenced. Alcoff (1990) argues that while it may not be politically effective to completely abandon the practice of speaking for those less privileged it must be done thoughtfully as it can increase the oppression of the group that is spoken for. The problem with these assumptions, and the main problem with the public criminology literature is the erasure of power and power relations that takes place therein. We are not all equally powerful as publics or as academics.

The rigid distinction between public criminology and Buraway's other three types limits criminology as a discipline. It forces our criminological work to remain untouched by the public by setting up a unidirectional flow of information and influence. Certainly in the public sociology literature, where the professional sociologist does the theoretical and analytic work of sociology and the public sociologist acts as a translator of that work and a messenger of it to different audiences, information can only flow from the discipline down to the public. If public criminology deals with the public then professional, critical and policy criminology does not. This means that we bring our knowledge to the public, but we never bring their knowledge, understandings, concerns, and strategies back to the discipline of criminology. This is not to suggest that academics should uncritically adopt public discourse as their own, but that they engage in dialogue rather than act as translators or messengers. The unidirectional transmission of knowledge implied in the public criminology literature limits its research and theoretical capabilities.

It also leads to problematic relationships between the public and scholars. Academics, working within the institutional constraints of universities and publishing industries, only allow the public access to and use of their work on terms dictated by that context. What power relations are sustained and bolstered here? The academy remains a privileged site, but does this mean that academics, the privileged, only bring their knowledge down to the less privileged public? If this is the case, then academics also bring their solutions to the problems of others (Acker 2005) rather than working with marginalized communities to generate materially situated and grassroots solutions.

Collins' approach is an intersectional one that is attentive to issues of power and belonging. Intellectual activism must therefore be an interactive process. Collins (2013) highlights the value and importance of engaging in "a public conversation of knowledge construction" (xix) rather than bringing knowledge to a passive public audience. Attention to power relations is central to the idea of intellectual activism; Collins (2013) argues that "by sharpening our focus on power and developing tools that enable us to see how its domains are organized and can be changed, our engaged scholarship creates space for change" (76). Collins' discussion of intellectual activism is always attuned to power differentials and one of her main points is to break down the binary between scholarship and activism. Rather than taking our cue from Buroway and the public sociology literature, a better frame for change making and social justice is intellectual activism. Utilizing a feminist approach such as Collins' can help us remain vigilant about the power relations of public engagement.

FEMINIST CAUTIONS AND FINAL THOUGHTS

Feminist criminology and sociology provide general cautions about doing change-making work. Feminist efforts at change making stand as a cautionary tale, that no matter how critical or transformative we want our impact to be, there are no guarantees that our efforts will not be put to different uses. Snider (2003) reminds us that feminist and other critical knowledge claims have been incorporated into the social reality we now wish to change and we must recognize our role in that process. For example, feminist and other critical knowledge claims were used to solidify the broader neoliberal move towards harsher punishment and hyper criminalization (Snider, 2006). Feminist calls for gender equality were translated into equality with a vengeance wherein women were seen as equally violent as men and deserving of equally harsh punishment[1] (Minaker & Snider, 2006). There is always the risk that "in a culture of punitiveness reforms will be heard in ways that reinforce rather than challenge dominant cultural themes; they will strengthen hegemonic not counter-hegemonic practices and beliefs" (Snider, 2003: 369). In order to understand the reception and impact of our ideas we need to examine the power relations into which they inserted (Snider, 2003). Intellectual activists need to ask who benefits, who is disadvantaged, whose interests are served and who has the power to adopt and use their knowledge claims (Snider, 2003). Power must be theorized in terms of knowledge production, engagement with different publics and the reception of ideas.

---

[1] Examples include the de-gendering of the language around violence against women to partner or family violence and mandatory arrest laws which saw increasing numbers of women arrested alongside the men who abused them.

Feminist reflections on media engagement, the main practice advocated by public criminology, illustrate these power issues. Feminists have many cautionary tales to share about this form of public engagement. Crocker (2010) analyses the media frenzy that took place around the Dating Violence on Campus study in the 1990s. This survey used a broad definition of abuse, including any "intentional physical, sexual, or psychological assault" on a woman by a male dating partner (Crocker, 2010) resulting in 81% of survey respondents reporting at least one form of abuse. The media frequently reported these results alongside scathing critiques of the definition of abuse and the measures used in the survey. Rather than raising the public's consciousness regarding the prevalence of violence against women this survey provided the media with an opportunity to dismiss feminist concerns as a moral panic.

Feminist work often speaks to and against deeply ingrained cultural values that critique the privilege held by dominant groups and strives to generate space for marginalized voices. At times, this results in feminism receiving a negative response from the media (Grauerholz & Baker-Sperry 2007). For example, Mopas and Moore (2012) describe their failed attempt to counter the sensational reporting of an on campus sexual assault with a more nuanced argument around the rarity of random, stranger attacks and the more common situation of intimate partner violence[2] (Mopas & Moore 2012). When the two academics attempted to counter sensational claims made by a colleague their expertise was belittled because they did not have the experiential knowledge the reporter was looking for, they could not say they had "ever sat across the table from a sex offender" (Mopas & Moore 2012). The resultant media storyline was not about the details and realities of sexual assault, instead it was about competing expert claims and expertise, with the opposing academic able to claim he spoke to the consensus among criminologists while "his detractors, reside outside the borders of criminology and therefore lack the authority to speak on criminal matters" (Mopas & Moore 2012: 189). Feminists

---

[2] They also detail their successful strategy of engaging directly, more as activists than experts, with the community at a vigil held at the university. This supports the contention that we need to conceptualize the change making work we do more broadly as intellectual activism.

have shown that engaging with media does not mean stepping into a neutral public dialogue, instead "larger socio-political forces, particularly backlash against feminism must be carefully acknowledged and evaluated" (Grauerholz & Baker-Sperry 2007, 281) whenever this type of public work is attempted.

A final caution from feminism is the recognition that scholars operate in institutional contexts that do not necessarily support public types of work. Feminist scholars have argued that no matter what type of public work scholars may wish to engage in, there are institutional barriers to doing so within academia (Sprague & Laube 2009). Graduate training, as currently structured, often impedes public work by focusing solely on basic research and training students to write and speak in a prescribed academic style at the expense of skills needed for public engagement. Feminists have pointed out the lack of prestige awarded to public work; if on a curriculum vitae at all, it occupies a more marginal position, which can be a problem for those looking to secure an academic position or who are working towards tenure (Mopas & Moore 2012). This is not an observation made by feminists alone. Currie (2007) identifies the privileging of original empirical research, the low status given to reports or trade publications, and disciplinary isolation as impeding the practice of public criminology. The problems of institutional recognition and support, however, may be heightened for scholars working from alternative and/or critical perspectives. These are institutional issues that cannot be ameliorated through individual action alone. Rather, these concerns are part of the broader context of knowledge production and the power relations therein.

In order to practice a public criminology that is transformative and radical we cannot accept the literature as currently formulated. A feminist analysis of public criminology reveals a glossing over of the many power relations that are present in the production of scholarship, engagement with the public and reception of our ideas. Transformation change making is an integral goal of feminism and we can build a more critical and transformative public criminology by addressing and incorporating some of these criticisms and suggestions.

References

Acker, Joan. 2005. "Comments on Burawoy on Public Sociology." *Critical Sociology*, 31(3): 327-331.

Alcoff, Linda. 1991. "The Problem of Speaking For Others." *Cultural Critique*, Winter 1991-92: 5-32.

Barak, Gregg. 2007. "Doing Newsmaking Criminology from Within the Academy." *Theoretical Criminology*, 11(2): 191-207.

Benhabib, Seyla. 1992. *Situating the Self: Gender, community and postmodernism in contemporary ethics.* New York: Routledge.

Burawoy, Michael. 2005. "For Public Sociology." *American Sociological Review*, 70(1): 4-28.

Burawoy, Michael. 2007. "For Public Sociology." In *Public Sociology: Fifteen Eminent Sociologists Debate Politics and the Profession in the Twenty-First Century*, eds. Dan Clawson, Robert Zussman, Joya Misra, Naomi Gerstel, Randall Stokes, Douglas Anderton and Michael Burawoy. Berkeley: University of California Press, 23-64.

Carrabine, Eamonn, Maggy Lee, and Nigel South. 2000. "Social Wrongs and Human Rights in Late Modern Britain: Social Exclusion, Crime Control, and Prospects for a Public Criminology." *Social Justice*, 27(2): 193-211.

Collins, Patricia Hill. 2013. *On Intellectual Activism*. Philadelphia: Temple University Press.

Collins, Patricia Hill. 2000. *Black Feminist Thought: Knowledge, Consciousness, and the Politics of Empowerment.* New York: Routledge.

Comack, Elizabeth. 1996. *Women in Trouble*. Halifax: Fernwood Publishing.

Comack, Elizabeth. 2006. "The Feminist Engagement with Criminology." In *Criminalizing Women*, eds. Gillian Balfour and Elizabeth Comack. Halifax: Fernwood Publishing, 22-54

Creese, Gillian, Arlene, McLaren, and Jane, Pulkingham. 2009. "Rethinking Burawoy: Reflections from Canadian Feminist Sociology." *Canadian Journal of Sociology*, 34(3): 601-622.

Crenshaw, Kimberle. 1991. "Mapping the Margins: Intersectionality, Identity Polictics, and Violence Against Women of Color." *Stanford Law Review*, 43(6): 1241-1299.

Crocker, Diane. 2010. "Counting Woman Abuse: A Cautionary Tale of Two Surveys." *International Journal of Social Research Methodology*, 13(2): 265-275

Currie, Elliott. 2007. "Against Marginality: Arguments for a Public Criminology." *Theoretical Criminology*, 11: 175-190.

Daly, Kathleen and Meda Chesney-Lind. 1988. "Feminism and Criminology." *Justice Quarterly*, 5(4): 407-538.

Doe, Jane. 2003. *The Story of Jane Doe: A Book About Rape*. Toronto: Random House.

Feilzer, Martina. 2009. "The Importance of Telling a Good Story: An Experiment in Public Criminology." *The Howard Journal*, 48(5): 472-84.

Fraser, Nancy. 1989. *Unruly Practices: Power, discourse, and gender in contemporary social theory*. Minneapolis: University of Minnesota Press.

Fraser, Nancy. 1990. "Rethinking the Public Sphere: A Contribution to the Critique of Actually Existing Democracy." *Social Text*, 25/26: 56-80.

Gal, Susan. 2004. "A Semiotics of the Public/Private Distinction." In *Going Public: Feminism and the Shifting Boundaries of the Private Sphere*, eds. Joan Scott & Debra Keates. Urbana: University of Illinois Press, 261-277.

Gotell, Lise. 2012. "Third-Wave Anti-rape Activism on Neoliberal Terrain: The Garneau Sisterhood." In *Sexual Assault in Canada: Law, Legal Practice and Women's Activism*, ed. Elizabeth Sheehy. Ottawa: University of Ottawa Press, 243-266.

Grauerholz, Liz, & Lori Baker-Sperry. 2007. "Feminist Research in the Public Domain: Risks & Recommendations." *Gender & Society*, 21(2): 272-294.

Hannah-Moffat, Kelly, and Margaret Shaw, eds. 2000. *An Ideal Prison? Critical essays on women's imprisonment in Canada*. Halifax: Fernwood Publishing.

Haraway, Donna. 1988. "Situated Knowledges: The Science Question in Feminism and the Privilege of Partial Perspective." *Feminist Studies*, 14(3): 575-599.

Hayman, Stephanie. 2006. *Imprisoning our Sisters: The new federal women's prisons in Canada*. Montreal & Kingston: McGill-Queen's University Press.

Hogeveen, Bryan, and Andrew Woolford. 2006. "Critical Criminology and Possibility in the Neo-liberal Ethos." *Canadian Journal of Criminology and Criminal Justice*, 48(5): 681-701.

Kramer, Ronald. 2009. "Resisting the Bombing of Civilians: Challenges from a Public Criminology of State Crime." *Social Justice*, 36(3): 78-97.

Land, Kenneth. 2010. "Who will be the Public Criminologists? How will they be Supported?" *Criminology & Public Policy*, 9(4): 769-770.

Levan, Andrea. 1996. "Violence against Women." In *Women and Canadian Public Policy*, ed. Janine Brodie. Toronto: Harcourt Brace and Co, 320-353.

Loader, Ian, and Richard Sparks. 2011. *Public Criminology?* New York: Routledge.

Loader, Ian, and Richard Sparks. 2010. "What is to be Done with Public Criminology?" *Criminology & Public Policy*, 9(4): 771-81.

McLaren, Margaret. 2002. *Feminism, Foucault and Embodied Subjectivism*. Albany: State University of New York Press.

Minaker, Joanne, and Laureen Snider. 2006. "Husband Abuse: Equality with a Vengeance?" *Canadian Journal of Criminology and Criminal Justice*, 48(5): 753-780.

Mopas, Michael, and Dawn Moore. 2012. "Talking Heads and Bleeding Hearts: Newsmaking, Emotion and Public Criminology in the Wake of a Sexual Assault." *Critical Criminology*, 20: 183-196.

Naffine, Ngaire. 1987. *Female Crime: The Construction of Women in Criminology*. Sydney: Allen and Unwin.

Razack, Sherene. 2002. "When Place Becomes Race." In *Race, Space and the Law: Unmapping a White Settler Society*, ed. Sherene Razack. Toronto: Between the Lines, 1-46.

Risman, Barbara. 2006. "Feminist Strategies for Public Sociology." In *Public Sociologies Reader*, eds. Judith Blau and Keri Smith. Lanham: Rowman & Littlefield Publishers Inc, 281-292.

Rock, Paul. 2010. "Comment on 'Public Criminologies'." *Criminology and Public Policy*, 9(4): 751-67.

Smart, Carol. 1995. *Law, Crime and Sexuality: Essays in Feminism*. London: Sage Publications.

Smith, Dorothy. 1987. *The Everyday World as Problematic: A Feminist Sociology*. Toronto: University of Toronto Press.

Smith, Dorothy. 1990. *The Conceptual Practices of Power: A Feminist Sociology of Knowledge*. Toronto: University of Toronto Press.

Snider, Laureen. 2006. "Making Change in Neo-liberal Times." In *Criminalizing Women: Gender and (In)Justice in Neo-liberal Times*, eds. Gillain Balfour and Elizabeth Comack. Halifax: Fernwood Publishing, 323-342.

Snider, Laureen. 2003. "Constituting the Punishable Woman: Atavistic Man Incarcerates Postmodern Woman." *British Journal of Criminology*, 43(2): 354-378.

Sprague, Joey, and Heather Laube. 2009. "Institutional Barriers to Doing Public Sociology: Experiences of Feminists in the Academy." *American Sociology*, 40: 249-271.

Stacey, Judith. 2004. "Marital Suitors Court Social Science Spin-sters: The Unwittingly Conservative Effects of Public Sociology." *Social Problems* 51(1): 131-145.

Tonry, Michael. 2010. "'Public Criminology' and Evidence-based Policy." *Criminology & Public Policy*, 9(4): 783-97.

Turner, Elizabeth. 2013. "Beyond 'Facts' and 'Values': Rethinking some Recent Debates about Public Role of Criminology." *British Journal of Criminology*, 53(1): 149-66.

Uggen, Christopher, and Michelle Inderbitzin. 2010. "Public Criminologies." *Criminology & Public Policy*, 9(4): 725-49.

On Some Limits and Paradoxes of Academic Orations on Public Criminology

NICOLAS CARRIER

> *Science (...) presupposes that what is yielded by scientific work is important in the sense that it is 'worth being known'. In this, obviously, are contained all our problems. For this presupposition cannot be proved by scientific means.*
> - Max Weber (1922[1946:143])

INTRODUCTION

There is now a significant and diverse contemporary academic literature revolving around the allegedly untapped potential that the social sciences (or social scientists' orations) present for acting upon modes of social organization and social relations, through their ability to enlighten or otherwise influence the beliefs and attitudes held by 'the public'.[1] This massive and ever growing literature has been described by Nickel (2010) as representing nothing less than a looming "public turn in the social sciences". Yet, typically, calls for de-cloistering academic communications to more directly target either 'the public' or specific 'publics' are made with regard to a singularized discipline. As such, they typically take the following form: 'for a public [enter discipline]'. One can thus read, in highly specialized peer-reviewed journals, articles on public sociology, public

---
[1] Thanks to Justin Piché for inviting me to contribute to this special issue. Thanks also to Augustine SJ Park, Dale C. Spencer and Jeffrey Monaghan for their comments on an earlier version of this article, as well as to my audience at the 3rd Critical Perspectives conference in Ottawa, where I first presented my critique of calls for public criminology.

philosophy, public ethnography, public history, public economics, public international relations, public anthropology, public criminology, and so on—something that Wacquant (2011) ridiculed as a disciplinary disease, that of "public-itis".[2] This article almost entirely limits itself to its criminological nosography.

Contributions on public criminology manifest themselves within highly specialized academic networks of communications. Most constitute interventions to stimulate its development. As will be critically discussed at greater length below, calls for public criminology typically start by lamenting the diminished influence of criminology, and by evoking an urgent need to reverse this trend, given what is usually referred to as the punitive turn characterizing contemporary liberal democracies. Not infrequently, contributions on public criminology take on a confessional path, recounting one's frustrating or heroic adventures in trying to be a public criminologist, hoping to provide roadmaps and warnings to an academic public confronted with the normative—rather than cognitive—injunction to 'go public'. Throughout this article I shall refer to this type of contributions as public criminology's 'cookbooks'.

Calls for public criminology suggest various forms of *division of criminological labour*, frequently begging for a greater academic recognition of criminologists' involvement in non-academic communication networks, particularly in the mass media. Criminologists are invited to embrace Marx's (1845) eleventh thesis on Feuerbach, to practice a form of criminology that is *relevant*, geared towards *having an impact* outside academia, particularly by making a difference in how people think and feel about criminological objects, and how sovereign power is exercised upon them. A repeated exhortation found in cookbooks is to use *a discourse that can easily travel* outside of academic frontiers. This article identifies some limits of the core qualities of academic orations on public criminology: the divi-

---

[2]Commenting on the emergence and solidification of debates surrounding the project to develop, nurture and assess public criminology, Wacquant (2011:439) felt the need to confess his instantaneous reaction: "I thought to myself, ''Not again! Another discipline struck by the disease of 'public-itis'", which occurs when you put the nice Habermassian-sounding qualifier 'public' in front of its name, in the quixotic belief that something new is thereby being discovered or argued."

sion of criminological labour, the diminished influence of criminology, the framework of relevance, the framework of transmission, and the framework of impact. In some cases, these limits can be observed as paradoxes folded into the work of the proselytizers. Such is the case, notably, in what I will call the paradox of mastery, where critics of social control show themselves obsessed with controlling and manipulating their fellow citizens, as well as in the paradox of exclusion, where critics of exclusionary policies advocate for public criminological discourses and engagements premised on the negation of the validity of certain criminological discourses. To be clear: my object is constituted by communications in the scientific system, not by the many utterances of academics outside academic communication networks. Whether or not the civic engagements of criminologists actually display the limits and paradoxes observable in academic calls for public criminology is a question that could inform future empirical research, and on which I shall not speculate in this article.

FROM PUBLIC SOCIOLOGY TO PUBLIC CRIMINOLOGY

In the case of academic contributions and debates related to public criminology, calls for a public criminology are mostly made through a discussion of, or superficial reference to, Burawoy's (e.g. 2005a, 2005b, 2004) division of sociological labour. Burawoy suggested distinguishing public sociology from three other forms of sociology. Like 'policy sociology', public sociology would concern itself mainly with an extra-academic audience. But whereas policy sociology is premised on an instrumental relation to knowledge, public sociology would be mobilizing a form of knowledge characterized by its reflexivity. 'Critical sociology' and 'professional sociology' constitute the two other types of sociology from which public sociology is distinguished. They both target an academic audience, and, here again, the distinction instrumental/reflexive knowledge would enable us to separate professional from critical sociology.

Burawoy's typology and call for public sociology have generated many debates and critiques, that he himself described as 'the public sociology wars' (2009).[3] Leaving aside the question

---
[3] For instance, Ericson (2005:371) has suggested that the absence of sociology "in some public spheres may actually be a positive sign that

of the influence that these debates have had and continue to have on the minds and practices of academics, it is clear that, to use Burawoy's types, they show the characteristics of professional and critical sociology: discussions and publications on public sociology take place through mediums targeting an academic audience, usually having to cross the borders policed by the peer-review process. That the same could happen to public criminology—that it could become a self-referential discussion amongst academics within academia—is a fear that has already been expressed by Loader and Sparks (2010a:18) in their influential *Public Criminology?*

The articulation of many discussions on public criminology to the model provided by Burawoy is made by silencing previous and different calls for public sociology, which did not insist, like Burawoy, on building a consensus between sociology/sociologists and various publics through the maintenance of hierarchical epistemologies. Moreover, they were not "focused on stabilizing and popularizing professional sociology" (Nickel, 2010:696). Prior to Burawoy's offensive, Agger (2000), Feagin (2001) and Gans (1989) called for a public sociology conceived as "a mode of writing that reveals that it is subjective authoring rather than an objective observation, [which] engages in self-translation with a public in mind, and addresses major public issues" (Nickel, 2010:695). Tittle (2004) has similarly noted, but from quite a different epistemological posture, that Burawoy's model hides or fails to recog-

---

sociology is maintaining its critical role". Tittle (2004) has mounted a severe critique of public sociology, equating it, among other things, with patronizing tendencies and dishonest sociological claims threatening to further reduce "what little legitimacy sociology has" (p.1639). If Burawoy (2005a:4) suggests that the four types of sociology entertain an "antagonistic existence", van Seters (2010:1149-1150) has noted how Burawoy "promotes the idea of public sociology as the discipline's crowning achievement: in public sociology, we need the distinctive qualities of the three other types, and these three feed into and support the distinctive quality of the fourth, not the other way around". Others have proposed critiques of public sociology from epistemological (e.g. Powell, 2012), feminist (e.g. Creese, McLaren and Pulkingham, 2009) and Marxist (Paolucci, 2008) perspectives. Still others, like Wacquant (2011) and Deflem (2013), have forwarded harsh personal attacks towards Burawoy, locating his campaign for public sociology within the nasty micro-politics of power in American sociological organizations. In a nutshell: the *academic* debates on public sociology are vivacious and sometimes vicious.

nize the fallibility of sociological knowledge. As such, the model that public sociology has oftentimes provided for criminology, through Burawoy's influence, is not one clearly premised on the intention to avoid the condescension of distributing epistemologies hierarchically.[4] Echoing anthropological and philosophical debates on the 'crisis of representation' (e.g. Marcus, 1998; Mienczakowski, 1996; Denzin, 1992; Clifford, 1986; Rorty, 1980), but also some variants of postmodernist criminologies and feminist criminologies (e.g. Hannah-Moffat, 2011; Chesney-Lind, 2006; Arrigo and Bernard, 1997; Daly, 1997; Pfohl, 1990; Pfohl and Gordon, 1986), these alternative conceptions of public sociology thus insisted on nurturing public discourses by presenting sociological knowledge as highly contestable, being eminently anchored in contingent assemblages of time and space. Thus, the fact that many, if not most, calls for public criminology are premised on a conception of the criminologist as the master of truth on crime and punishment is not without limitations and paradoxes.

PLURAL ORATIONS FOR PUBLIC CRIMINOLOGY

When compared to the intensity of debates on public sociology, public criminology has yet to become a strong polarizing theme in criminological academic communication networks. While critical discussions are certainly already observable, harsh and systematic critiques equivalent to Deflem's (2013) and Tittle's (2004) demolition of public sociology are difficult to locate. Nevertheless, critical voices are becoming less exceptional in the periphery of a growing constellation of academic productions chanting the potential of public criminology. I will discuss some of these discordant voices below. For now, I want to point out that behind the apparently consensual chorus of criminologists ready 'to go public' and 'to make a difference' is a (frequently unacknowledged) plurality of the very aims that ought to be those of public criminology.

The most discussed case is probably Loader and Sparks' call to "realize the unfulfilled promise of modern politics"

---

[4]It is thus unsurprising that feminists (e.g. Taylor and Addison, 2011:3) insisting on the "complexities of dialogue and listening" and on the "limits of writing" do not feel at ease with the project to 'go public' as championed by Burawoy.

(2010a:117). Stated slightly less abstractly, yet still equivocally, theirs is a call to see public criminology "contributing to better politics of crime and its regulation" (Loader and Sparks, 2011b:736; 2010a:117; 2010b:776). To do this, public criminologists are invited to embrace the ethics of the "democratic underlaborer". This figure, borrowed from Swift and White (2008), is said to be a politicized update of Locke's Enlightenment-era figure of the underlaborer, whose (philosophical) work enables or facilitates access to the (scientific) light of truth.[5] Following Loader and Sparks, the "criminologist as democratic underlaborer has a commitment both to generating and disseminating knowledge *and* to a more deliberative politics of big public questions such as the future of punishment and crime control" (2010b:779, their emphasis). They insist that "the public value of democratic under-laboring lies *not* in 'cooling' down controversies about crime and social responses to it, but in playing its part in figuring out ways to bring the 'heat' within practices of democratic governance" (2010a:132, their emphasis). Loader and Sparks (2010a:ch.4) thus clearly distinguish their call for public criminology from normative discourses advocating the insulation of penal policy from pressures stemming from 'the public' (e.g. Zimring and Johnson, 2006; Zimring, Hawkins and Kamin, 2001).

Other calls for public criminology are less focused on a celebration of the promises of deliberative democracy, yet still abide by a clearly modernist problematic, simply moving the focus of the celebration to the cognitive-instrumental rationality of science.[6] Arguing that "reliable knowledge" should be the in-

---

[5] In his *Essay Concerning Human Understanding*, Locke wrote: "The commonwealth of learning is not at this time without master-builders, whose mighty designs, in advancing the sciences, will leave lasting monuments to the admiration of posterity: but every one must not hope to be a Boyle or a Sydenham; and in an age that produces such masters as the great Huygenius and the incomparable Mr. Newton, with some others of that strain, it is ambition enough to be employed as an under-labourer in clearing the ground a little, and *removing some of the rubbish that lies in the way to knowledge*" (Locke, 1690[1975:9-10], my emphasis).

[6] It is common to distinguish the cognitive-instrumental, moral-practical and expressive-aesthetic rationalities (see, among others, Wagner [2008], Maffesoli [2008], Santos [2002], Touraine [1992], and Habermas [1976]). Criminological celebrations of the cognitive-instrumental rationality of science typically lead to underscore problems in the technical ordering of the

strument of social reforms (Matthews, 2009:356), dreaming of increased authority for criminology (as science) over penal policy (as a product of political power), such calls equate the need for public criminology with the need to "fight for" truth and against nonsense (Currie, 2007; see also Turner, 2013). Let me quickly provide some illustrations. In what is probably the first call for public criminology, Carrabine, Lee and South (2000:208) asked their academic audience to go public and to "popularize critical evidence", allowing for the "empowerment" of "the ordinary public" through sorting good and bad evidence and "emphasizing social justice and human rights", aiming to undo "social wrongs" and to promote "social rights".[7] Rowe (2012) suggests that a "priority" for public criminology "might be to more effectively establish the nature of the discipline in its sociological form" (p.35), as it would possess better access to the causes of crime, and could thus fight against the "misconceptualization of crime" (p.31), enabling a "more informed public discourse". Uggen and Inderbitzin (2010) consider that strengthening professional criminology is one of the aims of public criminology, so that science could more successfully erase the gap between "perceptions" and "evidence", and more fiercely fight against moral entrepreneurs[8] and moral panics: "potential for bias, uninformed demagoguery and political partisanship represent important pathologies that public criminologists must address head-on" (p.738). Similarly, Fichtelberg and Kupchik (2011:61) see criminologists as "experts with a unique contribution to make to debates on criminal justice policy", and believe that public criminology shall "enhance the credibility" of the 'discipline'. It is from this general perspective of crimin-

---

criminal legal system and to subsume questions of justice into questions of (scientifically valid) truths (see below).

[7] In contradistinction to many others, these authors do not see anything new here, but hope to re-vitalize these aims. They also note that their notion of public criminology is heavily indebted to Carlen's (1996) invitation to practice a 'political criminology'. Similarly, references to *The New Criminology* are found throughout Loader and Sparks' contributions, enabling them to insist on the political nature of crime.

[8] The authors are mobilizing an old and problematic objectivist-normative social problems theory (see Carrier, 2013), notably arguing that public criminology might "build interest in social problems" that do not exist as such for 'the public' (Uggen and Inderbitzin, 2010:738).

ology as the master of truth on crime and punishment that public criminology cookbooks are usually published (e.g. Rowe, 2012; Wilson and Groombridge, 2010; Feilzer, 2009; Groombridge, 2007).

Carrabine, Lee and South (2000) have alluded to the intimate proximity between public criminology and news-making criminology (Barak, 2007; 1988). Aspirant news-making criminologists are invited to hear Becker's (1967) scolding and to take sides, Barak (2007:204) seeing in the blogosphere the condition of possibility for anyone to "speak truth to power" and to "be heard doing so". He summarized news-making criminology in the following way:

> newsmaking criminology refers to the conscious efforts and activities of criminologists to interpret, influence or shape the representation of 'newsworthy' items about crime and justice. (...) It strives to affect public attitudes, thoughts and discourses about crime and justice so as to facilitate a public policy of 'crime control' based on structural and historical analyses of institutional development; allows criminologists to come forth with their knowledge and to establish themselves as credible voices in the mass-mediated arena of policy formation; and asks of criminologists that they develop popularly based languages and technically based skills of communication for the purposes of participating in the mass-consumed ideology of crime and justice (Barak, 2007:191-192).

Turner (2013) has suggested that news-making criminology should not be equated with either public criminology as a celebration of the promises of deliberative democracy (democratic underlaboring), nor with public criminology as a celebration of the cognitive-instrumental rationality of science (fighting for truth). News-making criminology would constitute a third form of public criminology.[9] Yet some public

---

[9] In her eyes, news-making criminology is a third form of public criminology notably because news-making criminologists "abandon any sense that different knowledge discourses can or should be able to gain traction in the world *except* through the maximization of opportunities for multi-mediated exposure" (Turner, 2013:159, her emphasis). Although one can perhaps agree that news-making criminology aims at influencing rather than educating the public in the way that, say, Currie advocates, Turner's typology falls short of satisfactorily providing criteria to distinguish news-making criminology from public criminology *à la* Loader and Sparks. Furthermore, she seems to suggest that because Barak is questioning the possibility of objective knowledge, news-making criminology is not premised on a correspondence theory of truth—something that can be easily debated considering Barak's

criminology cookbooks do not so sharply erect boundaries between democratic underlaboring, fighting for truth and making news. Let me take two examples. Piché's (forthcoming) confessional piece is about how, in his "capacity as criminologist", he tried to force greater governmental transparency in relation to the economic costs associated with the expansion of carceral spaces in Canada. It is about 'making news', it is about democratic underlaboring, and it is also about 'educating the public'. Mopas and Moore's (2012) confessional piece is (at least partly) about how one of their colleague managed (in their eyes) to promote fear in the wake of a sexual assault, while their own involvement in the mass media was allegedly not successful, something they try to explain by the fact that they wanted to adopt a detached and objective stance. They conclude by asking criminologists not only to go public, but to do so in a "more sensational" fashion, 'connecting' with 'the general public' at the level of emotions, and trying to "redirect (...) people's fear and anger [which are] legitimate reactions to crime (...) towards more productive ends" (Mopas and Moore, 2012:194,185). Here again, the boundaries between news-making and public criminology are not clearly drawn—and it is also not clear how engaging in an attempt at emotional manipulation outside of a clinical space can be associated with causing enlightenment or nurturing deliberative politics,[10] even when it is achieved by trying to mobilize criminological truth claims sensationally.

---

insistence to attend to historical and structural dimensions of institutional developments and to articulate mass mediated realities to bourgeois capitalist hegemony. It is also unclear how Barak's aim to nurture more "progressive" discourses on crime and criminal 'justice' differs from Loader and Sparks' aim to contribute to "better politics of crime and its regulation".

[10] The same could be said about other contributions. For instance, Kramer (2009/2010:89) sees the role of public criminology as contributing to "define certain harms as state crime and legitimate targets for social control efforts". Kramer's piece is unusual in that calls for public criminology are typically domestic in scope. But there is a pretty healthy form of "entrepreneurial criminology" that aims to claim its mastery over aspects of international relations increasingly described with the grammar of criminalization (see Carrier and Park, 2013).

Discordant Voices

The previous section showed that calls for public criminology are diverse and, to a certain extent, conflicting. Most are a celebration of either the cognitive-instrumental rationality of science or of the possibilities of democratic collective decision-making. Yet many contributions cannot be so easily discretely distributed, nor does adding news-making criminology to build a threefold typology enables a meaningful grasp of the internal complexity of the literature. Because of this internal complexity, some discordant voices focus on particular conceptions of public criminology, whereas others forward their critiques toward this fad in a less specified way.[11] I will present some of these critiques here, and introduce others further below, alongside my own discussion of contemporary orations for public criminology.

A general critical reaction of many criminologists has been to suggest that public criminology amounts to nothing more than a new label put on old and constant practices (e.g. Clear, 2010). This rebranding could, cynically or with some ire, be observed as a good way to satisfy "institutional demands for nonstop innovative publishing and (...) social relevance" (Carlen, 2011:97). A second general critical reaction has been to trouble the gospel of public criminology on its messianic evidence: from a narrowly scientist and epistemologically uncritical perspective, as Turner (2013:152) noted, one can advance "that much criminological work is 'bad science', and too many criminologists are engaged in ideological disputes and politically partisan projects, using inadequate methods and producing findings that are contradictory, controversial and out of touch with the needs of policy makers" (see also Rock, 2010). Although

---

[11] It remains to be seen whether or not one could simply transpose critiques of public sociology to public criminology, something which might appear warranted given that many criminologists, particularly British ones, tend to see criminology as an excrescence of sociology, typically silencing the vitality of sociologically ill-informed criminological practices and discourses. If one wanted to 'apply' some of Deflem's (2013) critiques of public sociology to public criminology, then one would suggest that public criminology is, among other things, the symptom of the marketization of the discipline (or field) which, having lowered its scientific standard and seeing graduation as a question of justice rather than of merit, is now populated with people too dumb to see that we need to save criminology from public criminology.

not speaking from such an uncritical perspective, Carlen (2011:98) has voiced her opposition to the "institutionalization of public criminology" on the grounds that "its proponents, instead of merely canvassing for others to join them in an avowedly political endeavour (about the desirability of their work having an effect beyond the academy) conflate their personal morality/politics with a scientific art form". A third general critique is not related to the weakness of criminological truth claims *per se*, but to the quite rudimentary or totally absent theorization of the *Realpolitik* of policy formation, let alone of political power (Tonry, 2010; Rock, 2010). A fourth general critique, formulated by Ruggiero (2012, 2010), amounts largely to a reformulation of Gouldner's (1975) classic critique of the criminologists as 'zoo-keepers', denouncing public criminology for being "missionary and paternalistic". Moreover, Ruggiero criticizes public criminology for being potentially unable to be strongly 'public', because criminology would try to operate, in terms of the theories/concepts it mobilizes, independently from sociology. Ruggiero himself advocates for a sociology of social movements à la Touraine, and suggests going beyond the "plea to be nice" (2012:157) that public criminologists would be addressing to policy-makers: we should be walking in the footsteps of giants like Hulsman and Mathiesen, embracing "abolitionism as public sociology".

Amongst the critiques specifically forwarded to Loader and Sparks' contributions, the strongest ones have converged on their "unarticulated" beatific and consensual conception of political power (Currie, 2011:72; see also Turner, 2013; Ruggiero, 2012; Sim, 2011). Emphasized here is the naive belief that politics is or can be governed by truth, an ingenuousness that critics have illustrated by evoking various 'pathologies' of current political institutions, sometimes even suggesting that deliberative democracy might be more a problem than the solution (see also Rowan, 2012). In a similar vein, Wacquant (2011:444) has lambasted the authors for failing to take into account the "political economy of the production, circulation and consumption of criminological knowledge", laughing at the presumption that criminological research is "conducted 'for the people' rather than for state managers". In the eyes of Christie (2011:709), Loader and Sparks not only downplay the dangerousness of the criminologists as experts, but also "make criminologists a bit too respectable—a breed of kind and useful helpers to our societies" that do not nurture enough a "quarreling society". Hammersley (2013) has proposed that Loader and Sparks' underlaborer is as falsely modest as Locke's underlaborer was. Others have criticized their injunction to be tolerant of the internal complexity of criminological practices and discourses, as if all forms of criminology could contribute to 'better politics of crime' (Tombs, 2011; Walters, 2011).

Some of these general and specified critiques will be revisited in discussing the limits and paradoxes that can be observed in the contemporary orations of public criminologists, to which I now turn. In my discussion, I shall frequently—hopefully not unduly—disrespect the internal complexity of the literature on public criminology and speak of it as a whole. This can be justified if one accepts that, irrespective of the political persuasions and epistemological postures of the proselytizers, which are typically not radical nor anarchistic, the unity of the calls for public criminology is located in the normative a priori that truth discourses should be either decisive or influential in the answers provided to questions of justice.

THE LIMITS OF THE CRIMINOLOGICAL DIVISION OF LABOR

Public criminology, we are told in many instances, is not for every criminologist. Loader and Sparks (2010a:6) indicate that they have no grudge with "criminologists who dedicate themselves inside the academy to a dispassionate, curiosity-driven search for knowledge and understanding of crime and justice", thus appearing to leave the "dispassionate scholar" outside the realm of public criminology (Walters, 2011). The dispassionate scholar is not invited to change what she is doing—particularly if she does not have what it takes to be in the media jungle—while criminologists who consider 'going public' are admonished to hone their communicational skills (Rowe, 2012; Currie, 2007), learning to practice a 'crime talk' that is "appropriate, relevant, and interesting" (Feilzer, 2009:482). Those who end up being "successful" in doing public criminology "necessarily will be generalists, widely educated" individuals, who shall "have to work to stay apprised of the latest research to be accepted as reliable experts or analysts" (Uggen and Inderbitzin, 2010:739). This seems to suggest that the public criminologist is not conceived as a producer of truth claims but as a popularizer—he would merely adapt and vulgarize complex narratives and data analyses, making them edible for a mass audience. Either mobilizing Burawoy's typology or developing new ones, calls for public criminology promote a definitive ceasefire amongst various forms of criminological practices, leaving a nice and supposedly respectable place for everyone. Loader and Sparks (2010a) thus suggest that the 'democratic underlaborer' can operate alongside the 'scientific expert', the 'policy advisor', the 'observer-turned-player', the 'activist' and the 'lonely prophet'.[12] And while "dancing with us all holding hands" (Walters, 2011:731), the proselytizers are asking (e.g. Currie, 2007) for a greater institutional recognition of the academic quality of their involvement in non-academic communication networks—an involvement which, to repeat, is distinguished from scholarly activities motivated by a will to understand.

In debates on public sociology, such attempts to divide the labor of social scientists have been ridiculed, notably by Ericson (2005), for they are based on the idea that some social scientific practices are not public. If meaning is premised on difference (e.g. Luhmann, 2002, 1999a, 1999b; Derrida, 1967), then public criminology is a category that makes no sense, as it does not allow us to distinguish different forms of criminologies. One could reply that public criminology is not replete with jargon and can be mass consumed; the modes of writing/speaking could thus offer themselves as a way to distinguish public and non-public criminologies.[13] Criminology stands accused of

---

[12] Wacquant (2011:) criticized this 'subjectivist' typology, of which the process of construction is not transparent, and confessed being "amused and bemused" of being slotted on a desert island as a 'lonely prophet'. He also pointed out that Loader and Sparks forgot to make room for the academic as 'grant manager', who produces graduate students and publishes largely by exploiting their labour.

[13] Outside of debates on public criminology, Christie reportedly confessed (Ruggiero, 2010:13) that his advice has always been: "when writing, keep your favorite aunt in mind". The argument is that social scientists have nothing to say about society that cannot be expressed colloquially—all the rest being, to speak colloquially, intellectual masturbation. The sophistication of specialized social theory language is sometimes condemned for its obscurity, but it is also defended as a necessity to meaningfully engage with

not having the intention to reach a wide audience, and it could be suggested that this goal enables us to separate public and non-public criminologies. But it is exactly here that we find one major limit of the calls for public criminology: they operate as if the public nature of criminology ought to reveal itself in the form of the popular. Bringing together Deflem's (2013) attack on public sociologists as "politicized populists" and Ruggiero's (2012) attack on public criminologists as limiting themselves to "pleas to be nice", we can see in the proselytizers' activities an injunction to develop a particular form of populist criminology: a 'be nice' populism that aims to oppose penal populism (Pratt, 2007; Bottoms, 1995), both sharing the same anti-intellectual proclivities. If criminologists can obviously oppose populism, one cannot oppose public criminology without opposing criminology itself.

The Limits of the Thesis of the Declining Influence and the Paradox of Exclusion

Contributions on public criminology are not the only set of academic communications to deplore the declining influence of criminological truth claims on penal policies, many seeing in penal populism or in the "punitive turn" symptoms of the inability of criminology to steer penal policies as it once did (see Carrier, 2010). Although these discourses are not devoid of normative underpinnings, they are to be located within an academic quest to make sense of various processes of "penal intensification" (Sim, 2009), and, as such, the diagnosis of the decline of influence has an analytical value, however debatable it might be. In contradistinction, the thesis of the decline of influence operates totally normatively within calls for public criminology. For

---

the complexity of the subject matter of social sciences (e.g. Teubner, 1989). But given that criminological productions are typically unencumbered by this kind of jargon, it is not the sophisticated language of social theory but the symbolic performance of scientific objectivity through the manipulation "off-putting cultural codes" that is seen as distancing "criminology from engaged public discourses" (Ferrell, Hayward and Young:2008:171). Ferrell, Hayward and Young provide some quotes from criminological journals that would be inadequate—dehumanizing—ways to talk about people, associating (some) criminological practices to vampirism, "systematically suck[ing] the life from those they describe". What is denounced is thus the "abstracted empiricism" (Mills, 1959) of criminological communications.

instance, Currie (2007:177) lamented that "our impact on the world outside ourselves has been nothing remotely like what it should have been, or needs to be", while Barak (2007:201) complained that, at least in the USA, "criminology does not get the respect it deserves". If only, complained Groombridge (Wilson and Groombridge, 2010; Groombridge, 2007), the public would think more "criminologically". Matthews (2009:341) decried the "inverse relationship between the expansion of academic criminology and its policy relevance", and it is along similar normative lines that Loader and Sparks (2010a:ch.1) see in criminology a "successful failure", positing an inverse relationship between the expansion of academic criminology and its influence.

One could be tempted here to repeat Hammersley's (2013) point on the false modesty of the 'democratic underlaborer', or perhaps even to speak of the proselytizers' delusions of grandeur. Like Tonry (2010), I submit the exact opposite interpretation: criminology has been, and continues to be, tremendously influential outside academic communication networks. The thesis of the decline of influence is unsatisfactory because of its implicit conceptual architecture, which limits the empirical manifestations of criminological influence to legislative activities, (penal) organizational practices and political discourses, and only when they align with the political persuasions of the criminologist mobilizing the thesis. All the utterly powerful social work of (what we can conveniently call) mainstream criminology, which continues to reproduce and further naturalize an ontological scission between sovereign power and crime, is totally silenced. None of the booming criminological research trying to locate the causes of crime in biological programs molded and contingently activated by the environment,[14] which is highly popular and frequently thematized by the mass media, is to be found in the contemporary orations for public criminology. Yet cookbooks are published by self-congratulatory public criminologists trying to reflect on the transient experience of having had the spotlights of a local newspaper turned towards them. None of the many tools used to sort, manage, predict—such as the 'Level of Service Inventory-Revised', an instrument developed by Canadian criminologists who have been instrumental in the revival of the quest for 'what works' in corrections—are seen as

---

[14] See Carrier and Walby (forthcoming, 2011), Walby and Carrier (2010).

a symptom of the influence of criminology, nor are they described as the achievements of public criminologists, even though they are supposed to be 'evidenced-based' (see Harcourt, 2007). This limited set of examples is sufficient to make visible that the thesis of the decline of influence is premised on the distinction between good and bad public criminology, only the good one being characterized by the trendy yet meaningless predicate of 'public'. This is particularly obvious in Mopas and Moore's (2012) lamentations about the alleged influence of their colleague, whose activities are not part of the celebration of public criminology, only because his criminological truth claims happen to differ from theirs, and because he was not attempting to manipulate emotions according to their conception of productivity.

This enables us to see the paradox of exclusion evoked in the beginning of the article: critics of exclusionary policies advocate for public criminological discourses and engagements premised on the negation of the validity of certain criminological discourses. This was perhaps already very clear in my discussion of public criminology as a celebration of the cognitive-instrumental rationality of science. From this neopositivist posture, obviously, distinguishing strong truth claims from weak or false ones can hardly be problematized (e.g. Carrabine, Lee and South, 2000); criminology would allow for the progressive, if painful, accumulation of knowledge, and public criminologists have a duty to help the public realize that some of their colleagues' work is rubbish. The problem arises for public criminologists adopting a more or less radical version of constructivism, without which crime remains ontologized. Not only can they not so easily brandish the currencies of truthfulness and falsehood while, speaking in their capacity of social scientists outside of academic communicational networks, they are nevertheless forced to do so. They also cannot, as Powell (2012:91) pointed out in relation to public sociology, "dismiss their opponents as mere ideologues" without undermining the legitimacy of their own truth claims.[15]

---

[15]The latter point has been the locus of criminological debates on postmodernism, which many criminological practices have resolved by opting for an "ethical" or "part-time constructivism" (see Carrier, 2006), enabling some criminological objects, such as harm or justice, to escape the supposedly debilitating sword of relativism. The anarchism of radical constructivism

THE LIMITS OF THE FRAMEWORK OF RELEVANCE

What is the meaning of the repeated yet vague injunction to be relevant within contributions on public criminology? In many calls for public criminology celebrating the cognitive-instrumental rationality of science—most particularly American ones—relevance seems to mean policy-relevance; that is, presenting elements that can be used by organizations, the legal system and the political system, perhaps also by families and individuals (e.g. crime prevention). Such a policy-relevant criminology is clearly pretty healthy, and no one really needs to stimulate criminological practices preoccupied by the issues preoccupying the middle classes (such as sexting, bullying, youth gangs, cybercrime, etc.), which are typically financially well-supported. For Rock (2010:755), the criminology that is "at risk of emaciation" is rather "a criminology that is not relevant in any commonplace, utilitarian meaning of the term, a criminology for which funds and public support are far less secure." He adds that "Universities are (...) one of the very few sanctuaries left" for those interested in producing forms of knowledge that are not in high demand and that might not be transformed into an instrument by capitalistic or political forces. Will public criminology tightens the already solidly established "structural coupling" (Luhmann, 2004, 1995) of criminology with the political and economic systems (see Walters, 2007, 2003)?

Perhaps we should understand the call for relevance as emanating from an 'engineering' perspective, criminology condemning itself to the impossibility to adopt an "overhanging perspective" through which it could perhaps grasp, and engage with, complex regimes of domination (Boltanski, 2009)? This latter role, as we saw, would be the fate of the 'lonely prophet'. Public criminologists should see that society makes productive use of the emotions generated by situations understood through the grammar of criminalization; they should provide tools to steer or shape state apparatuses' ways of inflicting pain and doing 'justice'; they should clear the ground so that 'the public' is not embarrassed by unnecessary complexities and doubts in its discussions, making possible a 'better politics of crime', etc. As

could certainly trouble many conceptions of (institutionalized criminal) 'justice' and of the 'legitimacy' of collectively binding decisions visible in contributions on public criminology.

Braithwaite (2010:223) remarked, the institutional success story of criminology can hardly be explained by its "intellectual achievements". An insistence on narrowly defined relevance is likely to increase "the empirical emasculation of theories" that was so ferociously denounced in *The New Criminology* (Taylor, Walton and Young, 1973: 278)—an oeuvre to which, interestingly enough, the 'democratic underlaborer' is supposedly attached. The division of labor advocated by public criminologists thus sets aside a place for allegedly irrelevant forms of scholarly activities, which in turn are used to establish the validity of truth claims of criminologists inviting their colleagues to busy themselves only with relevant stuff. If one chooses to emphasize an academic perspective rather than a political or managerial one (which certainly does not mean that the observer would then be operating outside a normative realm), the intellectual or cognitive relevance of public criminology is certainly hard to locate.

The Limits of the Framework of Transmission

Criminological work should not only be relevant, it should be easy to understand and easily disseminated by the mass media. Public criminologists' orations in non-academic communication networks should be sensational, or at least entertaining. Obviously, these injunctions are also articulated through the framework of impact; what I want to quickly convey before discussing impact is a constructivist argument which troubles the very notion of transmission mobilized by public criminology.

A constructivist epistemology does not conflate the identity of nominally shared objects with the identity of their meaning, nor does a social science built on this epistemological posture assume that the meaning given to an utterance (the meaning that you give to this very sentence, for example) is reducible to or deducible from it (Carrier, 2011, 2008a, 2008b). From such a posture, the meaning of increasing incarceration rates, for instance, is not posited as stable when it is a theme of communication (*i.e.* when it is a reality produced by) the political, legal, scientific, artistic, mass media, educational or economic social systems. Each of these social systems gives meaning to this fact differently, self-referentially, in a way that cannot be reduced to factuality (e.g. Luhmann, 2000, 1998). Many theoretical traditions in social sciences point out that the dichotomy between facts and values is a problematic one, but public criminology shows itself unable to accept the corollary that communication cannot be limited to factual elements.[16] To complicate matters further, we could operate within the phenomenological tradition, which insists on the importance of time in relation to meaning, and thus mobilize a concept of meaning that always synthesizes factual, social and temporal dimensions (Luhmann, 1995). This would notably lead us to consider quite simplistic the old input/output communicational model mobilized in public criminology, as well as its unarticulated, commonsensical, theorization of interpretation.[17] But such considerations are exactly the kind of conceptual work that many who call for public criminology either dismiss, seek to avoid, or they leave for the allegedly 'lonely ones' kindly authorized to stay busy with irrelevant stuff.[18]

THE LIMITS OF THE FRAMEWORK OF IMPACT AND THE PARADOX OF MASTERY

Loader and Sparks (2010b:778) have suggested that the democratic underlaborer is "committed, first and foremost, to the generation of knowledge rather than (first and foremost) scoring a point or winning a policy battle; if the distinction between criminologist and activist is to mean anything, then it must entail something of this kind". But one is left wondering how criminological *public-itis* could be so widespread without criminologists being seduced by the moral injunction to have an impact—a seduction that is perhaps stronger when calls for public

---

[16]See Turner's (2013) compelling analysis of Loader and Sparks' (2010a) debatable rapprochement between the 'democratic underlaborer' and Latour's (e.g. 2006, 1999) 'diplomat'.

[17]I formulate this critique from the perspective of social systems theory, although it could mounted from different theoretical angles, notably from Foucaultian, Habermassian, Bourdieusian and Boltanskian ones.

[18]This sometimes leads to surprising practices. For instance, Larsen wrote (Larsen and Piché, 2010) an academic article on the need to stop describing the Kingston Immigration Holding Centre (a Canadian carceral space seen as an instantiation of Agamben's (2005) *State of Exception*) as 'Gitmo North'. Yet, in one of the footnotes, we learn about the media coverage of the orations of Larsen who, as a public criminologist, tried to generate public outrage towards that space because it is 'Gitmo North'.

criminology take the form of a celebration of the cognitive-instrumental rationality of science. One way in which this preoccupation with impact manifests itself is through the proselytizers' critique (e.g. Currie, 2007) of peer-reviewed publications, which, in most cases, are read by a extremely small quantity of individuals. What is particularly condemned here is the self-referential nature of academic communications—criminologists talking to themselves and failing to go public. One limit or risk that the framework of impact presents is to propose a purely hetero-referential attribution of the value of academic truth claims. In other words, the risk is to replace the norms through which we can identify a form of communication as presenting the quality of scholarship by hetero-referential considerations, such as whether the communication is changing the attitude of the public, participating in effecting socio-political change, educating a public who does not think correctly, or manipulating a public that does not use its emotions productively.[19] When the framework of impact is mobilized by 'critical' criminologists (as we certainly cannot conflate public criminology with critical criminology), we can sometimes observe the paradox of mastery: critics of social control or moral panics adopt a normativity that define truth claims as good and valuable when they are effectively controlling others.

The framework of impact also manifests itself in the proselytizers' preoccupations with the lack of media training of current and future criminologists, and I wonder when the first public criminologist will follow the typical political manoeuvre of conducting focus groups in order to devise the most effective way to communicate with 'the public'. In calls for public criminology, the will to power takes over a will to interpret the reality of the mass media and the ways in which it interacts with criminological objects. Most (but by no means all) proselytizers

---

[19] The moral outrage that some public criminologists express towards the norms of the contemporary academic system and of academic organizations, such as the value placed on the quantity of peer-reviewed publications and on a purely quantitative appraisal of 'impact factor', is unlikely to compel Universities to revise their norms and to allocate value based on narrowly defined relevance, extra-academic popularity and impact. This contemporary academic normativity continues to offer itself as a support for the disrespect that many scholars show towards demands that non-academic activities be appreciated as an extension of scholarly activities.

somehow freeze the present of criminological knowledge, negate the importance of internal debates, strategically select and ignore elements of academic productions, and build various forms of 'be nice' populist discourses. One can certainly rejoice in seeing some criminologists inviting their fellow citizens to be gentle with each other and to work towards penal minimalism or penal abolitionism. What is nevertheless morally problematic is the a priori that a supposedly educated normative stance is superior to a supposedly uneducated normative stance. Criminologists can, for instance, go public and try to have an impact in making the public accept their truth claims on the little Utilitarian value that is to be found in mandatory minimum sentences. They can use non-academic tribunes to say something like: 'research shows they don't work—they do not reduce crime, they do not increase public safety, and besides they are costly and you are paying for it' (see Piché, forthcoming). But the superiority of consequentialism over retributivism cannot be established 'criminologically', as it cannot be established by a discourse that claims to be true and which is (at least) regarded as such within the self-referential communicational system of science. In other words: criminologists can pretend to know that a given course of penal action is likely to produce an outcome that they value or don't value, but they cannot find in academic truth claims the foundation or the legitimacy of such valuation. It is thus unsurprising that public criminology is ultimately forced to retreat into a moral argument blaming the ignorance of the others. One alternative to relying on morality in communication is "to cultivate uncertainty and the shared knowledge of ignorance" (Luhmann, 1998:100). Perhaps this alternative is unsuitable for contemporary forms of political communications, but it is certainly unlikely to seduce public criminology, as it rests on the negation of its own ignorance.

CONCLUSION

Among the themes silenced in contributions on public criminology is the limited accessibility of academic criminological communications published in peer-reviewed journals. Because of the frequent conflation of public with popular, the proselytizers tend to insist on strategies of dissemination that involves a transformation of academic discourses for mass consumption.

There is nothing inherently problematic about this, except considering this task as an academic rather than civic one. Such a project rests on the presumption that various publics have no interest in accessing academic communications in all their complexity and nuances or that they won't be able to make sense of them—a presumption which, in regards to many criminological productions, is, at very least, debatable. Can we find compelling reasons, given the current opportunities offered by communicational technologies, to justify the maintenance of an abject monetization of our articles in most peer-reviewed journals? For those who do not have access provided to them via organizational affiliation, the price of a single article is oftentimes superior to the cost of a criminological book. It is thus surprising that public criminologists are not currently engaged in the promotion of online, open access, peer-reviewed journals, which are still, in many circles, regarded as lacking prestige and peer recognition. Anecdotally, some colleagues refused to take part of this special issue on public criminology, preferring to get their article published in a less accessible journal, regarded as giving them more recognition, credibility and publicity. This illustrates the weight of the normativity of the scientific system on academic communications thematizing the normative injunction to go public, or, from Bourdieu's (2001) perspective, it illustrates how public criminologists cannot, as academic criminologists, escape the rules of the game through which 'scientific capital' is fought over and allocated.

Criminologists as social scientists cannot but continue to produce truth claims that conform to the norms of criminology as subsystem of science, without which their truth claims would be undistinguishable from non-scientific ones. This, obviously, does not mean that criminological truth claims are truer than other ones, but only that their truth value is established by the self-referential operations of the academic system which, one has to assume, "put to work situations and processes of decision which cannot be reduced to a simple exercise of belief and authority" (Berthelot, 1998:187, my translation).[20] From a constructivist perspective, this means that a scientifically territori-

---

[20] Obviously, academic individuals will oftentimes experience differently the peer-review process when its outcome is negative and appears to them poorly justified.

alized practice like criminology "has to make true propositions about the impossibility of truth" (Moeller, 2012:49). Whether they are regarded as the best true propositions (until further notice, as Giddens (1990) likes to add) or as interpretations (see Bauman, 1992), we cannot presume that the truth value granted by the scientific localization of discourses will be accepted by citizens and other social systems. Critics of Loader and Sparks, for instance, pointed out how politics oftentimes exhibit little respect for science.

Criminologists have very little control, if any, on whether their truth claims will be appropriated by citizens and social systems. Nor can they control, should this appropriation happen, the peculiar interpretation or "productive misreading" (Teubner, 1993) that shall be made of what they communicated. The proselytizers' apparent conjecture that presence in the mass media equals greater impact is farcical at best. Particularly when he tries to hide under truth claims his own conception of justice, the criminologist following public criminology cookbooks can hardly escape the fate of being constructed as a representative of yet another interest group, thus seeing his critique of penal policies getting "dissolved in the sea of ordinary critiques that go along with relations between groups, and which constitute the thread of the everyday life of politics, in its broad sense" (Boltanski, 2009:21; my translation). One alternative is a civic engagement that neither takes criminology for the master of truth nor rests on the democratic underlaborer's pretense that his truth claims are a condition for deliberations on justice. Such an alternative could mean, as Foucault (1984b) suggested[21], to speak on the grounds of a

---

[21] Foucault's political engagements were ultimately always justified by nothing more than his own subjectivity (in the same way that his intellectual work was articulated to his own self-transformation; see notably Foucault [1984c]). This has been made particularly clear, I think, in the beautiful and generous book written by his friend Paul Veyne (2008). See notably Veyne's short anecdote on Foucault's reaction to a television coverage of the Israeli-Palestian conflict, that Veyne uses to illustrate Foucault's "individual decisionism" in the realm of political action: *quand c'est insupportable, on ne supporte plus* ("when it is unbearable, we can no longer tolerate") and "jabbering" about reasons can "at best be useful in terms of rhetoric or propaganda" (Veyne, 2008:180; my translation). Always absent in Foucault's political engagements is the need to prove that his positions are just, that they are the right ones, that they are anchored in a scientific truth. In this regard, to

solidarity established by our common condition of being governed.

References

Agamben, G. 2005. *State of Exception*. Chicago: University of Chicago Press.

Agger, B. 2000. *Public Sociology: From Social Facts to Literary Acts*. New York: Rowman & Littlefield.

Arrigo, B.A. & T.J. Bernard. 1997. "Postmodern Criminology in Relation to Radical and Conflict Criminology." *Critical Criminology* 8: 38–60.

Bauman, Z. 1992. *Intimations of Postmodernity* New York: Routledge.

Barak, G. 2007. Doing Newsmaking Criminology from Within the Academy." *Theoretical Criminology* 11: 191-207.

Barak, G. 1988. "Newsmaking Criminology: Reflections on the Media, Intellectuals, and Crime." *Justice Quarterly* 5: 565-587.

Berthelot, J.-M. 1998. *L'intelligence du social*. Paris: Presses universitaires de France.

Boltanski, L. (2009). *De la critique. Précis de sociologie de l'émancipation*. Paris: Gallimard.

Bottoms, A. 1995. "The Philosophy and Politics of Punishment and Sentencing." Clarkson, C. and R. Morgan, eds. *The Politics of Sentencing Reform*. Oxford: Clarendon, 17-50.

Bourdieu, P. 2001. *Science de la science et réflexivité. Cours du Collège de France. 2000-2001*. Paris: Raisons d'agir.

Braithwaite, J. 2000. "The New Regulatory State and the Transformation of Criminology." *British Journal of Criminology*, 40: 222–238.

Burawoy, M. 2009. "The Public Sociology Wars." V Jeffries, ed. *Handbook of Public Sociology*. New York: Rowman & Littlefield, 449-473.

Burawoy, M. 2005a. "For Public Sociology." *British Journal of Sociology* 56: 259-94.

Burawoy, M. 2005b. "The Critical Turn to Public Sociology." *Critical Sociology* 31: 313-326.

Burawoy, M. 2004. "Public Sociologies: Contradictions, Dilemmas, and Possibilities." *Social Forces* 82: 1603–1618.

Carlen, P. 2011. "Against Evangelism in Academic Criminology: For Criminology as a Scientific Art." Bosworth, M. and C. Hoyle, eds. *What is Criminology?* New York: Oxford University Press, 95-110.

---

espouse Foucault's perspective is to abandon the desire to lay down the law for others and to try "to mold the political will of others" (Foucault, 1984a:1495; my translation).

Carrabine, E., M. Lee & N. South. 2000. "Social Wrongs and Human Rights in Late Modern Britain: Social Exclusion, Crime Control, and Prospects for a Public Criminology." *Social Justice* 27: 193-211.

Carrier, N. 2013. "De la problématisation des usage(r)s de drogues illicites." Otero, M. and S. Roy, eds. *Qu'est-ce qu'un problème social aujourd'hui? Repenser la non-conformité*. Québec: Presses de l'Université Laval, 249-277.

Carrier, N. 2011. "Critical Criminology Meets Radical Constructivism." *Critical Criminology* 19: 331-350.

Carrier, N. 2010. "Anglo-Saxon Sociologies of the Punitive Turn: Critical Timidity, Reductive Perspectives, and the Problem of Totalization." *Champ pénal/Penal Field. New International Journal of Criminology* 7 [online]: http://champpenal.revues.org/7952

Carrier, N. 2008a. *La Politique de la stupéfaction. Pérennité de la prohibition des drogues*. Rennes: Presses universitaires de Rennes.

Carrier, N. 2008b. "Speech for the Defense of a Radically Constructivist Sociology of (Criminal) Law." *International Journal of Law, Crime and Justice* 36: 168-183.

Carrier, N. 2006. "Academics' Criminals. The Discursive Formations of Criminalized Deviance." *Champ pénal/Penal Field New International Journal of Criminology*, 3 [online]: http://champpenal.revues.org/document3143.html

Carrier, N. & A.S.J. Park. 2013. "On an Entrepreneurial Criminology of Mass Political Violence." *Crime, Law and Social Change*, 60: 297-317.

Carrier, N. & K. Walby. forthcoming. "Ptolemizing Lombroso: The Pseudo-Revolution of Biosocial Criminology." *Journal of Theoretical and Philosophical Criminology*

Carrier, N. & K. Walby. 2011. "Putting Claims about the 'New Paradigm' of 'Biosocial Criminology' in Context" *Journal of Contemporary Criminal Justice* 27 (1) [online]: http://ccj.sagepub.com.proxy.library.carleton.ca/content/suppl/2011/11/08/27.1.81.DC1/Walby_and_Carrier_2010.pdf

Chesney-Lind, M. 2006. "Patriarchy, Crime and Justice: Feminist Criminology in an Era of Backlash." *Feminist Criminology* 1: 6-26.

Christie, N. 2011. "Reflections from the Periphery." *British Journal of Criminology* 51: 707-710.

Clear, T.R. 2010. "Editorial Introduction to "Public Criminologies"." *Criminology & Public Policy* 9: 721-724.

Clifford, J. 1986. "On Ethnographic Allegory." Clifford, J. and G.E. Marcus, eds. *Writing Culture. The Poetics and Politics of Ethnography*, Berkeley: University of California Press, 98-121.

Creese, G., A.T. McLaren & J Pulkingham. 2009. "Rethinking Burawoy: Reflections from Canadian Feminist Sociology." *Canadian Journal of Sociology* 34: 601-622.

Currie, E. 2011. "Thinking About Criminology." *British Journal of Criminology* 51: 710-713.

Currie, E. 2007. "Against Marginality. Arguments for a Public Criminology." *Theoretical Criminology* 11: 175-190.

Daly, K. 1997. "Different Ways of Conceptualizing Sex/Gender in Feminist Theory and their Implications for Criminology." *Theoretical Criminology* 1: 25-51.

Deflem, M. 2013. "The Structural Transformation of Sociology." *Society* 50: 156-166.

Denzin, N.K. 1992. *Symbolic Interactionism and Cultural Studies. The Politics of Interpretation*. Cambridge: Blackwell.

Derrida, J. 1967. *L'écriture et la différence*. Paris: Seuil.

Ericson, R. 2005. "Publicizing Sociology" *British Journal of Sociology* 56: 365-372.

Feagin, J. 2001. "Presidential Address. Social Justice and Sociology: Agendas for the Twenty-First Century." *American Sociological Review* 66: 1-20.

Feilzer, M. 2009. "The Importance of Telling a Good Story: An Experiment in Public Criminology." *The Howard Journal of Criminal Justice* 48: 472-484.

Ferrell, J., K. Hayward & J. Young. 2008. *Cultural Criminology: An Invitation*. London: Sage.

Fichtelberg, A. & A. Kupchik. 2011. "Democratic Criminology: The Place of Criminological Expertise in the Public Sphere." *Journal of Theoretical and Philosophical Criminology* 3: 57-88.

Foucault, M. 1984a. "Le souci de la vérité." Defert, D. and F. Ewald, dir. *Michel Foucault - Dits et écrits - II - 1976-1988*, Paris: Quarto, 1487-1497.

Foucault, M. 1984b. "Face aux gouvernements, les droits de l'homme." Defert, D. and F. Ewald, dir. *Michel Foucault - Dits et écrits - II - 1976-1988*, Paris: Quarto, 1526-1527.

Foucault, M. 1984c. "L'intellectuel et les pouvoirs." Defert, D. and F. Ewald, dir. *Michel Foucault - Dits et écrits - II - 1976-1988*, Paris: Quarto, 1566-1571.

Gans, H.J. 1989. "Sociology in America: The Discipline and the Public." *American Sociological Review* 54: 1-16.

Giddens, A. 1990. *The Consequences of Modernity*. Stanford: Stanford University Press.

Gouldner, A. 1975. *For Sociology*. Harmondsworth: Penguin.

Groombridge, N. 2007. "Criminologists say ... An Analysis of UK National Press Coverage of Criminology and Criminologists and a Contribution to the Debate on "Public Criminology"." *The Howard Journal of Criminal Justice* 46: 469-475.

Habermas, J. 1976. *Connaissance et intérêt*. Paris: Gallimard.

Hammersley, M. 2013. "Review of *Public Criminology?*" *Sociology* 47: 208-210.

Hannah-Moffat, K. 2011. "Criminological Cliques: Narrowing Dialogues, Institutional Protectionism and the Next Generation." Bosworth, M. and C. Hoyle, eds. *What is Criminology?* New York: Oxford University Press, 440-455.

Harcourt, B.E. 2007. *Against Prediction: Profiling, Policing, and Punishing in an Actuarial Age*. Chicago: University of Chicago Press.

Kramer, R.C. 2009/2010. "Resisting the Bombing of Civilians: Challenges from a Public Criminology of State Crime." *Social Justice* 36: 78-97.

Larsen, M. & J. Piché. 2009. "Exceptional State, Pragmatic Bureaucracy, and Indefinite Detention: The Case of the Kingston Immigration Holding Centre." *Canadian Journal of Law & Society* 24: 203-229.

Latour, B. 2006. *Changer de société - refaire de la sociologie*. Paris: La Découverte.

Latour, B. 1999. *Politiques de la nature. Comment faire entrer les sciences en démocratie*. Paris: La Découverte.

Loader, I. & R. Sparks 2011a. "Criminology's Public Roles: A Drama in Six Acts." Bosworth, M. and C. Hoyle, eds. *What is Criminology?* New York: Oxford University Press, 17-34.

Loader, I. & R. Sparks. 2011b. "Criminology and Democratic Politics: A Reply to Critics." *British Journal of Criminology* 51: 734-738.

Loader, I. & R. Sparks. 2010a. *Public Criminology?* London: Routledge.

Loader, I. & R. Sparks. 2010b. "What is to be Done with Public Criminology?" *Criminology & Public Policy* 9: 771-781.

Locke, J. 1690. *An Essay Concerning Human Understanding*. Nidditch, P.H., ed. New York: Oxford University Press, 1975.

Luhmann, N. 2004. *Law as a Social System*. Oxford: Oxford University Press.

Luhmann, N. 2002. *Theories of Distinctions. Redescribing the Descriptions of Modernity*. Stanford: Stanford University Press.

Luhmann, N. 2000. *The Reality of the Mass Media*. Stanford: Stanford University Press.

Luhmann, N. 1999a. "The Paradox of Form." D. Baecker, ed. *Problems of form*. Stanford: Stanford University Press, 15-26.

Luhmann, N. 1999b. "Sign as Form." D. Baecker, ed. *Problems of form*. Stanford: Stanford University Press, 46-63.

Luhmann, N. 1998. *Observations on Modernity.* Stanford: Stanford University Press.

Luhmann, N. 1995. *Social Systems.* Stanford: Stanford University Press.

Maffesoli, M. 2008. *Après la modernité? La logique de la domination. La violence totalitaire. La conquête du présent.* Paris: CNRS Éditions.

Marcus, G.E. 1998. "What Comes (Just) After "Post"? The Case of Ethnography." Denzin, N.K. and Y.S. Lincoln, eds. *Handbook of Qualitative Research - I - The Landscape of Qualitative Research.* Thousand Oaks: Sage, 383-406.

Marx., K. 1845. "Theses on Feurbach." Arthur, C.J. ed. Marx, K. and F. Engels. *The German Ideology. Part One with Selections from Parts Two and Three and Supplementary Texts.* New York: International Publishers, 121-123, 1970.

Matthews, R. 2009. "Beyond 'So What?' Criminology. Rediscovering Realism." *Theoretical Criminology* 13: 341-362.

Mienczakowski, J. 1996. "An Ethnographic Act. The Construction of Consensual Theatre." Ellis, C. and A.P. Bochner, eds., *Composing Ethnography. Alternative Forms of Qualitative Writings*, Walnut Creek: Altamira Press, 244-264.

Mills, C.W. 1959. *The Sociological Imagination.* New York: Oxford University Press.

Moeller, H.-G. 2012. *The Radical Luhmann.* New York: Columbia University Press.

Mopas, M. & D. Moore. 2012. "Talking Heads and Bleeding Hearts: Newsmaking, Emotion and Public Criminology in the Wake of a Sexual Assault." *Critical Criminology* 20: 183-196.

Nickel, P.M. 2010. "Public Sociology and the Public Turn in the Social Sciences." *Sociology Compass* 4: 694-704.

Paolucci, P. 2008. "Public Sociology, Marxism, and Marx." *Current Perspectives in Social Theory* 25: 353-382.

Pfohl, S. 1990. "Welcome to the PARASITE CAFE: Postmodernity as a Social Problem." *Social Problems* 37: 421–442.

Pfohl, S. & A. Gordon. 1986. "Criminological Displacements: A Sociological Deconstruction." *Social Problems*, 33: S94–S113.

Piché, J. forthcoming. "Playing the "treasury Card" to Contest Prison Expansion: Lessons from a Public Criminology Campaign." *Social Justice.*

Powell, C. 2012. "How Epistemology Matters: Five Reflexive Critiques of Public Sociology." *Critical Sociology* 39: 87-104.

Pratt, J. 2007. *Penal Populism.* New York: Routledge.

Rock, P. 2010. "Comment on "Public Criminologies"." *Criminology & Public Policy* 9: 751-767.

Rorty, R. 1980. *Philosophy and the Mirror of Nature.* Princeton: Princeton University Press.

Rowan, M. 2011. "Democracy and Punishment: A Radical View." *Theoretical Criminology* 16: 43-62.

Rowe, M. 2012. "Just Like a TV Show: public Criminology and the Media Coverage of 'Hunt for Britain's Most Wanted Man'." *Crime Media Culture* 9: 23-38.

Ruggiero, V. 2012. "How Public is Public Criminology?" *Crime, Media, Culture* 8: 151-160.

Ruggiero, V. 2010. *Penal Abolitionism.* New York: Oxford University Press.

Santos, B. de S. 2002. *Toward a New Legal Common Sense, 2nd ed.* London: Butterworths.

Sim, J. 2011. "Who Needs Criminology to Know Which Way the Wind Blows?" *British Journal of Criminology* 51: 723-727.

Sim, J. 2009. *Punishment and Prisons: Power and the Carceral State.* London: Sage.

Swift, A. & S. White. 2008. "Political Theory, Social Science, and Real Politics." Leopold, D. and M. Stears, eds. *Political Theory: Methods and Approaches.* New York: Oxford University Press, 49-69.

Taylor, I., P. Walton & J. Young. 1973. *The New Criminology: For a Social Theory of Deviance.* London: Routledge.

Taylor, Y. & M. Addison. 2011. "Placing Research: 'City Publics' and the 'Public Sociologist'." *Sociological Research Online* 16: 1-10.

Teubner, G. 1992. "The Two Faces of Janus: Rethinking Legal Pluralism." *Cardozo Law Review* 13: 1443-1462.

Teubner, G. 1989. "How the Law Thinks: Toward a Constructivist Epistemology of Law." *Law & Society Review* 23: 727-757.

Tittle, C.R. 2004. "The Arrogance of Public Sociology." *Social Forces* 82: 1639-1643.

Tombs, S. 2011. "Which Public? Whose Criminology?" *British Journal of Criminology* 51: 727-730

Tonry, M. 2010. ""Public Criminology" and Evidence-Based Policy." *Criminology & Public Policy* 9: 783-797.

Touraine, A. 1992. *Critique de la modernité.* Paris: Fayard.

Turner, E. 2013. "Beyond 'Facts' and 'Values'. Rethinking Some Recent Debates about the Public Role of Criminology." *British Journal of Criminology* 53: 149-166.

Uggen, C. & M. Inderbitzin. 2010. "Public Criminologies." *Criminology & Public Policy* 9: 725-749.

van Seters, P. 2010. "From Public Sociology to Public Philosophy: Lessons for Law and Society." *Law & Social Inquiry* 35: 1137-1154.

Veyne, P. 2008. *Foucault. Sa pensée, sa personne.* Paris: Albin Michel.

Wacquant, L. 2011. "From 'Public Criminology' to the Reflexive Sociology of Criminological Production and Consumption." *British Journal of Criminology* 51: 438-448.

Wagner, P. 2008. *Modernity as Experience and Interpretation. A New Sociology of Modernity.* Cambridge: Polity.

Walby, K. & N. Carrier. 2010. "The Rise of Biocriminology: Capturing Bodily Economies of 'Criminal Man'." *Criminology & Criminal Justice* 10: 261-285.

Walters, R. 2011. "Public or Civic Criminology: A Critique of Loader and Sparks." *British Journal of Criminology* 51: 730-734.

Walters, R. 2003. "New Modes of Governance and the Commodification of Criminological Knowledge." *Social & Legal Studies* 12: 5–26.

Walters, R. 2007. "Critical Criminology and the Intensification of the Authoritarian State." A. Barton, K. Corteen, D. Scott & D. Whyte, eds. *Expanding the Criminological Imagination: Critical Readings in Criminology.* Portland: Willan, 15-37.

Weber, M. 1922. "Science as a Vocation." H.H. Gerth and C. Wright Mills, eds. *From Max Weber: Essays in Sociology.* New York: Oxford University Press, 1946, 129-158.

Wilson, D. & N. Groombridge. 2010. "'I'm Making a TV Program Here!': Reality TV's *Banged Up* and Public Criminology." *The Howard Journal of Criminal Justice* 49: 1-17.

Wright Mills, C. 1959. *The Sociological Imagination.* New York: Oxford University Press.

Zimring, F & D. Johnson. 2006. "Public Opinion and the Governance of Punishment in Democratic Political Systems." *Annals of the American Academy of Political and Social Science* 605: 265–280.

Zimring, F., G. Hawkins & S. Kamin. 2001. *Punishment and Democracy: Three Strikes and You're Out in California.* New York: Oxford University Press.

[arts & culture]

Prisoner's Justice Day
(a retrospective montage[1])

"We can't change prisons without changing society; we know that this is a long and dangerous struggle. But the more who are involved in it, the less dangerous, and the more possible it will be."
(Claire Culhane's letterhead of the PRISONERS' RIGHTS GROUP)

It is said to have begun in Millhaven Maximum Penitentiary in Bath, Ontario on August 10th 1975, when prisoners refused to work or eat for the day in honor and remembrance of Edward Nalon, who had bled to death in an administrative segregation cell on August 10th 1974.

◄ original image from 1975, artist unknown, but it was created by a prisoner at Matsqui Medium Security Prison, BC.

"[That day, he] was expecting to be given the news that he was to be released from solitary confinement. The guards neglected to tell him of his pending release. [He'd been in segregation for more than a month, much of it in spent in 'the hole' on a restricted diet.]

---

[1] Compiled by pj lilley

Out of frustration or despair, he cut the vein in his inner elbow. The cells were equipped with call buttons that could be used to summon the guards in an emergency. He pushed the button in his cell, other prisoners pushed their buttons, nobody responded, and he bled to death.

An inquest into his death found that the guards had deactivated the call buttons in the unit. There were a number of recommendations made by the coroner's jury, including the immediate repair of the emergency call system.

On the first anniversary of Eddie's death, prisoners at Millhaven refused to work, went on a one day hunger strike and held a memorial service, even though it would mean a stint in solitary confinement. Many of the alleged leaders in this one day peaceful protest would still be in segregation a year later.

In May 1976, another prisoner, Bobby Landers died of a heart attack in the same unit. He tried to summon help but the call buttons had still not been repaired. Medical testimony at the inquest into his death established that he should have been in intensive care, not solitary confinement."

[He had been involuntary transferred to Millhaven on account of his activism in Archambault Penitentiary in Quebec.]

Prisoners at Millhaven put out a call for August 10th to be a national day of protest against an apathetic prison system that did not seem to care if people in prison lived or died."

> "On **Aug 10, 1976** thousands of prisoners across Canada staged a one day hunger and work strike in honour of Edward and Robert and since then August 10th has become a traditional day of remembering prisoners who died inside across Canada and internationally."

[The histories above are quoted from *'Prisoners' Justice Day from 1975 to 2013: Stories from Inside and Out'* (August 9, 2013) by the QPIRG-Concordia collective and from various notes on "Prisoner Justice Day" by PJD Committee in *Out of Bounds* (Vol.22, #2, Summer 2005, June print) by the prisoners at Williams Head federal prison and from the website <prisonjustice.ca>]

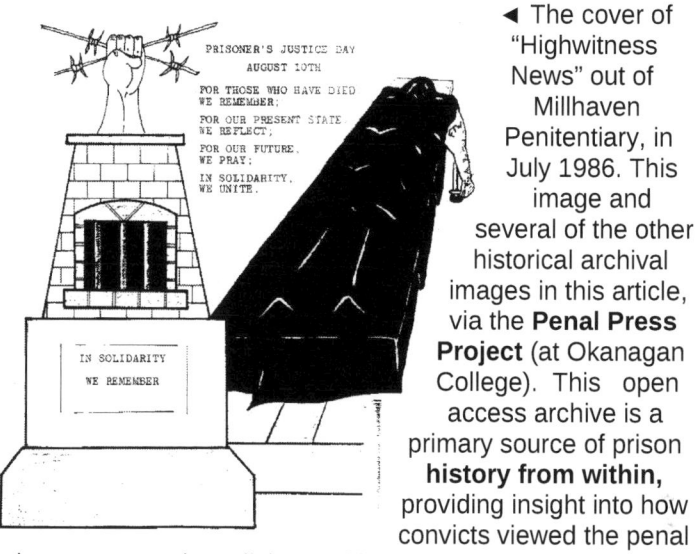

◀ The cover of "Highwitness News" out of Millhaven Penitentiary, in July 1986. This image and several of the other historical archival images in this article, via the **Penal Press Project** (at Okanagan College). This open access archive is a primary source of prison **history from within,** providing insight into how convicts viewed the penal justice apparatus, its policies and its practices. Thanks to Prof. Melissa Munn (and students) for diligence in scanning and indexing these newsletters, and to Dr. Robert Gaucher for his dedication over years of collecting, preserving and cataloging these important public records.

In his insightful historical account (1991[2]) of the Odyssey Group, and how the various prisoner committees built the initial momentum that first spread PJD recognition, Robert Gaucher writes

> The political consciousness and struggles of Canadian prisoners has been either denied or ignored by Canadian criminologists and social scientists. The slow, grinding struggles characteristic of the process of advancing prisoners' rights have also led some prisoners to devalue their political struggles as pointless or unproductive. However, in the tradition of the penal press, prisoners continue to reach outside the walls to educate and radicalize the public vis-à-vis the nature of criminal justice and penal oppression. Contemporary groups such as "Infinity Lifers" (1986-1991) at Collins Bay

---

[2] Gaucher, Robert. "Organizing Inside: Prison Justice Day (August 10th) A Non-Violent Response to Penal Repression" in the *Journal of Prisoners on Prisons, Vol. 3 Number 1 & 2 Autumn, 1990/ Spring, 1991: Capital Punishment & Prison Justice Day*

Penitentiary and "The Justice Group" (1987-1991) at Stony Mountain Penitentiary, represent this tradition. The success of the Odyssey Group's Prison Justice Day initiative exemplifies the outside directed nature of prisoner politics and the ability of prisoners to effect change. It should give strength to prisoners and their outside supporters and encouragement in their struggles for rights and against penal oppression.

This image, by Frank Borg, was the cover of the August 10th 1988 magazine *Out of Bounds* created inside Williams Head Prison. [via the Penal Press archive: http://penalpress.com/wp-content/uploads/OOB_Volume1No4JulAug1988.pdf]

As the stories, reflections, poems, and artwork spread by the penal press across to other (mostly the maximum-security) prisons, the observation of the memorial also spread. It was not just a memorialization, but a resistance, a demand for change, and an assertion of previous victories won through struggle, so of course, this was recognized as a threat by the prison authorities.

In the first few years, administrative reprisals were harsh against those hunger striking and refusing to work on August 10. Besides facing stints in segregation for their participation, organizers, as well as newsletter editors, and even artists and contributors often were transferred to a different institution after speaking out.

But, as Gaucher (1991[3]) describes, it continued to grow, and,

> By 1979, virtually all federal maximum security prisons were solidly represented and the proportion of federal prisoners taking part continued to grow through 1981. This was paralleled by growing national recognition and support outside the prison walls. Claire Culhane's Prisoners' Rights Group of Vancouver, Marrianne Rox, the Prisoners' Rights Group of Montréal and the Civil Liberties Association of Ottawa continued to provide publicity and organize major events in their areas, while smaller demonstrations of support sprang up in other cities. The Law Union organized Toronto's first public demonstration of support in 1978, and laid the basis for the tradition in that city [often outside the Don Jail.] Increasingly, outside support took the form of vigils and demonstrations outside prisons, including press conferences and the presentation of briefs outlining prisoners' concerns and demands.

After years of harassment of those prisoners who took part in PJD, including the loss of privileges and 'good' time for the general prison participants, and segregation and kidnapping (i.e., involuntary transfers) for the leadership, in 1988 the senior management committee of CSC decided to eliminate the practice of issuing 'performance notices', although those who refused to work were still docked a day's pay (*Tightwire*, 1988:15). Some members of Odyssey are on the street and doing well, some are still doing time. Prison violence and prisoners' deaths continue. Last month (March, 1991), ten women in the segregation unit of Kingston Prison for Women engaged in a hunger strike in response to the suicides of six Native prisoners in the past eighteen months and the institution's repression of the prison population's grief and anger.

> Aboriginal women inside the prison have endured not only the violence and oppression a patriarchal society forces on women, but also the genocidal campaigns of our white supremacist state in its attempts to conquer the Indigenous peoples of Turtle Island. The resistance of Feb. 6 (1991) was a response among the Native women and their sisters inside the walls to the death just days before of their sister and the racist and vile attempts of

---

[3] *ibid*

the prisoncrats to blame the death on Native women and on the Native services which elders provide (*Through The Walls*, "Press Release", March 6, 1991).[4]

▲ "Keep your spirit strong" • Prison Justice Day • by Gord Hill [1999?]

DECARCERATION & DECOLONIZATION

"I hope that people will take the 10th to think about, not only the people in prisons and the history of prisons, prison organizing and resistance, but also the way prisoners' justice and resistance against prisons intersects with the fight for justice for missing and murdered Indigenous women, for the victims of police murder, and for all families and communities struggling against the ongoing racist legacies of colonialism and capitalism that continue to attack us everyday." (Alex Hundert, preface to his statement to the court at sentencing as part of his G20 'main conspirators' case conviction.[5])

Indigenous women have borne a particularly heavy carceral burden as a direct result of the devastating legacy of colonialism which has attacked their spiritual and cultural (as well as economic and political) traditions at the foundation, and which continues to cause brutal dislocations, isolation, poverty and abuse.

---

[4] As quoted in: Gaucher, Robert. "Organizing Inside: Prison Justice Day (August 10th) A Non-Violent Response to Penal Repression" in the *Journal of Prisoners on Prisons*, Vol. 3 Number 1 & 2 Autumn, 1990/ Spring, 1991: Capital Punishment & Prison Justice Day

[5] Hundert, Alex. "For Prisoners Justice Day I am finally posting my Sentencing Statement from June 26, 2012" From his blog, Narrative Resistance, Aug. 8, 2013. http://alexhundert.wordpress.com/2013/08/08/for-prisoners-justice-day-i-am-finally-posting-my-sentencing-statement-from-june-26-2012/

Many First Nations historically have operated on a matrilineal system where descent is traced through the mother, meaning that a child would become a member of his or her mother's clan. Many societies were also matrilocal, in which a man married into a woman's family and would live with her community, resulting in settlement patterns based on the female line. In contrast, European settlers had taken for granted that a family was structured with men as the head of the family and the women as subservient, and tried to understand Aboriginal families by imposing a patriarchal European family model onto matriarchal Aboriginal kinship systems. This belief was perpetuated throughout government policies that attempted to restructure the Aboriginal family to fit this mould. Aboriginal kinship systems were forcibly restructured over time through a number of policies, including the Indian Act, Indian status, and the residential school system."[6]

The settler-colonialists also imposed their patriarchal Victorian moral values through the sexual policing of Indigenous women, and the construction of "deviance". As Gaucher explained,

[both above by Gord Hill]

> These concepts were written right into the Indian Act, with certain rights afforded to men and women of "good moral character," as determined by the Indian agent. The Indian agent became, therefore, a sort of sexual policing agent. Indian agents had the power to act as justices of the peace or magistrates, giving them legal authority to monitor and control their Indian charges. Any sexual relations that did not conform to monogamy in marriage were seen as un-civilized and counter to the government's civilizing mission.

---

[6] "A Brief History of the Marginalization of Aboriginal Women in Canada". 2009. First Nations Studies Program at the University of British Columbia. http://indigenousfoundations.arts.ubc.ca/home/community-politics/marginalization-of-aboriginal-women.html

Scholar Joan Sangster points out that female sexuality was regulated in numerous ways, with colonial law as "one crucial site of sexual regulation." The Indian Act gave the agent power to jail people, and the agent's responsibility for registering births, marriages, and those eligible for Indian status gave agents power to punish those who did not conform. While many First Nations customary laws allowed for divorces, Indian Agents forbade them. A woman cohabitating with a new partner could be charged with bigamy and sent off to a reformatory, far from her family and homeland. As Sangster points out,

> The fact that the Indian Affairs filing system designated a whole category for 'Immorality on the Reserves,' with almost all the complaints centering on sexual misbehavior, indicates the importance of the agent's role as custodian of sexual morality.[7]

As explained by INCITE, it was a similar process in the US context:

> "Native peoples' experiences of law enforcement violence are often com-

▲ by Neal Freeland. [2005] Cover art for Vol 18, #1-2 of the *Journal of Prisoners on Prisons* (2009). They say:

[T]he medium is pen and ink. The picture shows a man leaning against the bars, with cuffs on his wrists. It was originally drawn in 1995 and used for T-shirts in Stony Mountain Institution. The piece has since been redrawn with additional shading details using newer pen and inks.

"Neal Freeland is a Saulteaux artist and poet who spent 17 years in prison, and is currently living in the city, going to college, as well as continuing to work on his graphic novels and poetry."

Read more of him, and view other major artworks & commentary at their "Artists Guild" page: http://www.jpp.org/Coverart.html

---

[7] As quoted in: Gaucher, Robert. "Organizing Inside: Prison Justice Day (August 10th) A Non-Violent Response to Penal Repression" in the *Journal of Prisoners on Prisons*, Vol. 3 Number 1 & 2 Autumn, 1990/ Spring, 1991: Capital Punishment & Prison Justice Day

pletely erased from mainstream discussions of police brutality and immigrant rights.

Yet, since the arrival of the first colonists on this continent, Native women and Native Two Spirit, transgender and gender non-conforming people have been subjected to untold violence at the hands of U.S. military forces, as well as local, state and federal law enforcement. Movement of Native peoples across borders with Canada and Mexico has been severely restricted, often by force, separating families and communities. The notion of "policing" was forced on sovereign nations and cultures that had previously resolved disputes within communities."—**INCITE**: *Policing Native Women & Native Two Spirit and Trans People*"[8]

◄ Artist: BobbyLee Worm, (for PJD, 2012) As an Indigenous woman and residential school survivor, she further suffered through the trauma of domestic violence. Convicted in 2006, she was sentenced to 6 years, but she spent nearly 4 years locked in solitary confinement at the Fraser Valley Correctional Institution. In 2013, she won a civil suit (with the help of the BCCLA) against the government for its use of long-term "Management Protocol" (administrative segregation).[9]

So now, we are in a situation here where, according to the Canadian state's own 2013 statistics,

[w]hile Aboriginal people make up about 4% of the Canadian population, as of February 2013, 23.2% of the federal inmate population is Aboriginal (First Nation, Métis or Inuit)...The incarceration rate for Aboriginal adults in Cana-

---

[8] http://www.incite-national.org/page/policing-native-women-native-two-spirit-and-trans-people

[9] Her case, which includes extensive details on the physical, psychological and social effects of isolation and segregation (was aka 'Management Protocol') is reprinted here: http://bccla.org/wp-content/uploads/2012/03/20110303-BCCLA-Legal-Case-BobbyLee-Worm.pdf & after the court settlement: https://bccla.org/tag/bobby-lee-worm/

da is estimated to be 10 times higher than the incarceration rate of non-Aboriginal adults.

The over-representation of Aboriginal people in Canada's correctional system continued to grow in the last decade. Since 2000-01, the federal Aboriginal inmate population has increased by 56.2%. Their overall representation rate in the inmate population has increased from 17.0% in 2000-01 to 23.2% today ... Aboriginal women are even more overrepresented than Aboriginal men in the federal correctional system, representing 33.6% of all federally sentenced women in Canada.[10]

Yet, as bad as the statistics are, they don't convey how and why these horrors still keep playing out. The experience is often referred to as a 'double punishment', being Indigenous and a woman, but it adds up to a multiplicity of penalization: judges order on average longer sentences, and when the women get inside, they're usually given higher security risk assessments. Though solitary confinement is known to trigger depression, trauma and self-harm, the terrible truth is they are subjected to more frequent 'disciplinary' segregration time (23.5 hour/day lockdown/isolation) and much more frequent (than the 'average') administrative segregation (more than 45 days, 'indefinite' length isolation time.) This situation is actually significantly *worsening*—in the past decade more than ever before. According to the Ontario Women's Justice Network,

> [T]he effects of colonisation, assimilation, and systemic discrimination against Aboriginal peoples are still being experienced today, especially by Aboriginal women. These effects increase women's vulnerability to poverty, addiction, physical and sexual violence; this is reflected in the Aboriginal women offender population, where 90% of the women in prison report experiences with physical and/or sexual abuse ...[11]

---

[10] Office of the Correctional Investigator, *Backgrounder: Aboriginal Offenders—A Critical Situation*, (Office of the Correctional Investigator, 16 September 2013), online: http://www.oci-bec.gc.ca/cnt/rpt/oth-aut/oth-aut20121022info-eng.aspx

[11] "Over-Represented and Over-Classified: Crisis of Aboriginal Women in Prison". June 2014. *Ontario Women's Justice Network*, http://www.owjn.org/owjn_2009/jasons-test-submenu-page/367

◄ Image by Gord Hill (2007)

In Memory of Harriet Nahanee (Thitspa7s | Tseybayotl) Dec. 7, 1935–Feb. 24, 2007
She came from the Pacheedaht, who are part of the Nuu-chah-nulth peoples, and she married into the Squamish nation. She was a residential school survivor who became an activist for Indigenous rights and environmental justice. Harriet was sentenced to two weeks in a provincial jail in January 2007 for 'criminal contempt of court' for her part in the protest against the Sea-to-Sky Highway expansion (for the Olympics) at Eagleridge Bluffs. She died after developing pneumonia, which was attributed to the brutal cold concrete conditions in Surrey Pre-trial detention centre.

In Canada, (as under most other states), the majority of women in prison arrive there having been criminalized for some act of self-defense. This is especially the situation for Indigenous women, who are

> 3.5 times more likely than non-Aboriginal women to be victims of violence; and Aboriginal women between the ages of 25-44 are 5 times more likely to die from acts of violence than other women the same age.[12]

They are detained and arrested more frequently, and

> Aboriginal women are put into segregation more often and for longer periods of time than other offenders. ...

> Aboriginal women are more likely than non-Aboriginal women to report the most severe forms of spousal abuse. 54% of Aboriginal women report having been choked, beaten, threatened with a weapon like a gun or knife, and sexually assaulted by their partner.

---

[12]*Ibid,* based on information from Amnesty International, "Stolen Sisters: A Human Rights Response to Discrimination and Violence against Indigenous Women in Canada", (2004), online:
http://www.amnesty.ca/sites/default/files/amr200032004enstolensisters.pdf

> Most women who are charged for a violent offence like murder were defending themselves or their children from partner-violence. When an Aboriginal woman is charged with a crime, the discrimination that put her at risk of experiencing violence and offending in the first place, also impacts how the justice system and other institutions treat her. Aboriginal women are more likely to be sentenced to a prison term than any other population in Canada.[13]

#ItEndsHere #ItStartsWithUs

It is for all these reasons and more that the prison abolition movement has always been strongly tied to the Indigenous resurgence movement. More and more prisoners, activists and artists are beginning to walk on that path, joining in struggles that are connected to the defense of land and water, and to traditional (and often women and elder-led) social structures and practices; they assert that it is only through grassroots processes of transformative and restorative justice that any measure of healing can be achieved.

Or, as artist Erin-Marie Konsmo put it, "Ceremony *as* harm reduction".[14]

> via âpihtawikosisân > "It might not seem political to do art or ceremony...but it's important as Indigenous ppl to do that work and name the violence." #IW2SHRC [Indigenous Women & Two-Spirit Harm Reduction Coalition] [15]

In their collaborative response to the calls for a national enquiry by some family members of the hundreds of missing and murdered Indigenous women, the activist groups Families of Sisters in Spirit (FSIS)[16], No More Silence (NMS)[17] and the

---

[13] *Ibid*, based on information from Aboriginal Corrections Policy Unit, *Marginalized: The Aboriginal Women's experience in Federal Corrections*, by Mandy Wesley (Ottawa: Public Safety Canada, 2012), online: Public Safety Canada at
http://www.publicsafety.gc.ca/cnt/rsrcs/pblctns/mrgnlzd/mrgnlzd-eng.pdf

[14] From the conference *waniskâtân nîtisânitik: Indigenous Feminist and Two-Spirit Resistance on Turtle Island*
(https://www.facebook.com/events/375002092649806/)

[15] https://twitter.com/apihtawikosisan/status/515634081498152961

[16] Families of Sisters in Spirit (FSIS): https://www.facebook.com/pages/Families-of-Sisters-in-Spirit/169989823049052

Native Youth Sexual Health Network (NYSHN)[18] came together "to name the specific forms of state violence", and then express their frustration with the limitations of state grievances and "sham" inquiries:

[Artwork by: Erin Marie Konsmo, Media Arts Justice and Projects Coordinator, Native Youth Sexual Health Network]

> [M]uch of the violence we face as communities, nations, and families stems from colonial nation-states like Canada and the US and the laws themselves. Structures of colonialism (i.e. state governments, foster care, prisons, social services) are responsible for and contribute to ongoing violence against Indigenous women, girls, Two Spirit, and lesbian, gay, bisexual, transgender, transsexual, queer, questioning intersex, and asexual (LGBTTQQIA) people.[19]

They say they've "gone through 'the proper channels' and it hasn't got us any closer to justice that we are seeking." That instead, they would

> prefer to look to each other for solutions. Where we have seen success has been in engagement with people on the front-lines and in our communities who live these realities everyday and seek change. This is where we draw our strength. ...
>
> Collaboratively we are interested in nurturing self-determined and community-led solutions to interpersonal and structural violence. This is where our hearts are; in resistance

---

[17] No More Silence: https://www.facebook.com/pages/February-14-National-Day-of-Action-No-More-Silence/126403794094498

[18] Native Youth Sexual Health Network (NYSHN): http://www.nativeyouthsexualhealth.com/

[19] FSIS, NMS & NYSHN, "It Starts With Us" on the Indigenous Nationhood Movement blog, March 14, 2014. http://nationsrising.org/it-starts-with-us/

to colonialism and in fostering our solutions as Indigenous peoples with the support and consensual allyship of our non-Indigenous friends and family members in the struggle.[20]

They then proceed to outline several specific "examples of on the ground responses to deaths, disappearances and gender based violence" and how each of these can play out in practice is elaborated upon in their statement:[21]

> How to foster resurgence in everyday ways to respond to gender-based violence? Resurgence is working from our strengths and cultures as Indigenous nations and communities.
> 1. We need to lift each other up and support each other's well being.
> 2. Teach-ins and critical education with families and communities.
> 3. Media Arts Justice.
> 4. Centering Indigenous youth leadership and intergenerational organizing.
> 5. Supporting people in the sex trade.
> 6. Community-led database.
> 7. Local initiatives.
>
> **#ItEndsHere #ItStartsWithUs**
> **#Support Not Stigma**

Similar grassroots solutions are proposed in the "Organizing for Community Accountability Fact Sheet" produced by INCITE [22]

> "Developing community-based responses to violence is one critical option. Community accountability is a community-based strategy, rather than a police/prison-based strategy, to address violence within our communities. Community accountability is a process in which a community—a group of friends, a family, a church, a workplace, an apartment com-

---

[20] ibid

[21] Ibid.

[22] Community Accountability Fact Sheet and Tool Kit. INCITEblog.wordpress.com and at http://www.transformativejustice.eu/wp-content/uploads/2010/06/6685_toolkitrev-cmtyacc.pdf

plex, a neighborhood, etc—work together to do the following things:

- Create and affirm VALUES & PRACTICES that resist abuse and oppression and encourage safety, support, and accountability

- Develop sustainable strategies to ADDRESS COMMUNITY MEMBERS' ABUSIVE BEHAVIOR, creating a process for them to account for their actions and transform their behavior

- Commit to ongoing development of all members of the community, and the community itself, to TRANSFORM THE POLITICAL CONDITIONS that reinforce oppression and violence

- Provide SAFETY & SUPPORT to community members who are violently targeted that RESPECTS THEIR SELF-DETERMINATION"

◄ Artist: Michelle Commisso Pesce, PJD 2012

"All Prisoner Justice Day T-shirt designs were to be approved at the national level. The design this year had featured a fallen angel; wings outstretched with her face covered by her forearms, which were covered in scars. It drew attention to high rates of self-mutilation and suicide in the prison system, but also spoke to the potential of those who have fallen. But once national supervisors reviewed the T-shirt design, a new national directive was handed down: there would be no Prisoner Justice Day T-shirts."[23]

---

[23] Anonymous. "On a Precipice: Reflections on Prisoner Justice Day on the cusp of Bill C-10". Aug 16, 2012. Halifax Media Co-op: http://halifax.mediacoop.ca/fr/story/precipice/12144

Obviously, the increasing repression of free speech & expression isn't just about t-shirts, or even just books, art and the right to organize around greivances—a whole host of new controls and "cost-cutting" measures were imposed with the Conservatives' Bill C-10: charging prisoner's room and board; upping the costs of telephone access; and generally limiting access to creative materials and learning opportunities. The Harper Conservative government even made it a point to shut down all six of the prison farms (where 300 prisoners had worked).

"Canadians are being silenced on more and more issues," said Dianne Dowling, a Save our Prison Farm member and former leader of the group, in a statement. "From prison farms to pipelines to climate science, we need to stand against the silencing and stand for the well-being of our communities and our country."[24]

All these measures are being implemented while literally billions of dollars are being pumped into building new US Republican-style "superprisons" all across the country. In 2011, Alex McLelland of the Prison Moratorium Action Coalition wrote about the $1.1billion pricetag on the construction of the massive Toronto South Detention Centre:

As Justin Piché, a renowned critic of the federal and provincial "tough on crime" agenda, has noted, the cost of this new prison is so great that "those of us in our late twenties... will still be paying for the construction of this facility well into our fifties and its operation likely until the day we die."

Piché's research[25] has found that these new institutions are being developed based on the argument that the "prison population is no longer a homogeneous population," meaning: politicians and corrections bureaucrats need a way to deal with the increasing number of women, undoc-

---

[24] MacAlpine, Ian. "Prison farm protestors appeal to be heard Friday" in the Kingston Whig-Standard On-line, Jan. 30, 2014. → http://www.thewhig.com/2014/01/30/prison-farm-protestors-appeal-to-be-heard-friday

[25] Piché, Justin. "Tracking the Politics of Criminalization and Punishment in Canada" at tpcp-canada.blogspot.ca/2011/02/canada-at-crossroads.html

umented people, those with mental health issues, and drug users who are being incarcerated, not to mention the many indigenous peoples who have always been overrepresented in Canada's prisons.[26]

The earlier anonymous report from Halifax on Prison Justice Day in the women's federal prison continued:

> As one woman put it: "All over Canada, they are building and building, but you can't hide suicides with fancy new rooms".
>
> Funds spent on ballooning renovation budgets and increased numbers of prisoners has led to under-staffing. Everything from fewer programs due to lack of staff support to constant mail mix-ups creates dangerous levels of stress and upset amongst inmates. The complaint process is woefully inadequate. Staff don't have the time nor the training to help women resolve disputes. Women are frustrated.
>
> "We might as well not even have a complaint process," said another inmate. "They convince and intimidate women to sign it off as 'resolved' when it is not resolved. Admin doesn't want the correctional investigator to see it."
>
> It is likely that there will be a lot happening in Canadian prisons over the next few years that Federal departments wouldn't want an independent investigator to see. As we talked, the women lamented how, in just a few short years, the Harper government has decimated the positive changes that were made following public outcry over the events that took place at the Kingston Prison for Women in 1994. Prisoner Justice Day is the one day a year when prisoners come together to talk about injustice and those who have died. Given the swiftness with which our current Federal government has moved to undo years of progress in prison justice, it's no wonder they moved swiftly to cancel Prisoner Justice Day T-shirts. It is likely they were terrified of a riot. And available evidence suggests that they should be.
>
> When I asked the women what they would have talked about if a Prisoner Justice Day event had taken place that evening,

---

[26] McLelland, Alex. "More Jail Than We Need." in the *Torontoist*, March 17, 2011. http://torontoist.com/2011/03/a_superjail_in_toronto/

they responded with stories of men and women they had known who had died in prison, most of them by suicide. One woman said:

> "I would have shared a poem in honour of Ashley, a woman in her early twenties who stuck to my side like glue in the remand centre, simply because it was my idea to make an apple crisp out of the kitchen scraps. Ashley wanted to belong and be safe and when she didn't feel those two things, she wanted to die. In segregation, she died alone after drinking a bottle of toilet sanitizer. She was being filmed on suicide watch, but it was too late. She died while they watched."[27]

▶ ["Hang Rope" by Peter Collins, 2004.]

In his conclusion to his poignant, disturbing account of how Ashley Smith died, Don Weitz writes[28]:

> It's also significant that CSC's [Correctional Service Canada] mental health professionals as well as most of the inquest lawyers didn't try to deconstruct "mental disorder" or "mental illness" as attempts to cope with personal life crises. Together with psychiatrists and other mental health professional witnesses, they failed to understand that "mental health treatment" in prisons really means fraudulent psychiatric diagnoses, forced drugging, physical restraints, daily degradation and humiliation.

Ashley's suicide, like many other prisoner deaths, was not accidental, it was predictable and preventable.

---

[27] Anonymous. "On a Precipice: Reflections on Prisoner Justice Day on the cusp of Bill C-10". Aug 16, 2012. Halifax Media Co-op: http://halifax.mediacoop.ca/fr/story/precipice/12144

[28] Weitz, Don. "How Canada's Prisons Killed Ashley Smith: A National Crime and Shame" in Mad in America: Science, Psychiatry, and Community, December 14, 2013. http://www.madinamerica.com/2013/12/canadas-prisons-killed-ashley-smith-national-crime-shame/

He ends with the warning:

> The Harper government's "get tough on crime" policy that legislates building more prisons, overcrowding ("double-bunking"), mandatory and longer prison sentences have undoubtedly contributed to the epidemic of self-harm, suicide and violence in virtually all federal prisons in Canada. What's needed is not "prison reform" but prison abolition and community alternatives which were denied Ashley and many of her sister prisoners. There are and will be many other Ashley Smiths—a national shame and crime.[29]

NO DEATH IN PRISON IS A NATURAL DEATH

Artist and long-term prisoner Peter Collins has contributed a number of uniquely gut-wrenching pieces to the memorial of PJD. About it, he writes in his blog:

> August 10th is now the **International Memorial Day** for people who died while in the forced custody of the state, whether they were transgender, men, women, or children. Whether they were labelled criminal or political and whether medical negligence, beating, abuse, disease, old age, shock treatment or experimentation killed them, we solemnly remember. Whether it was a heart attack, overdose, shooting, gassing, asphyxiation, stabbing or state execution that killed them, we remember. Whether starvation, electrocution, hanging, murder, or suicide stopped their hearts, we remember. Prisoners and their families, friends and loved ones observe their suffering and their passing.
>
> There is **no natural death in prison** and there is no exclusion from the August 10th memorial if they died in custody.[30]
>
> ▶ ANGORR #019226 [2012][31]

---

[29] *Ibid.*

REMEMBERING TOGETHER

The outward expressions of PJD, the arts and poetry, have always been a central aspect of the process of remembering and passing it along. But there is also a constantly evolving struggle over the observance of the day, as some parts of it have become "accepted routine" by prison wardens. Certain practices, like making t-shirts featuring artwork for the day, have even become "institutionalized" although this is a highly contested process, as the approvals can be taken away on a whim, as happened in 2010...

▶ On our Radical Criminology cover, this image was cover of the prison press newsletter, *Cell Count* (Issue #66, Summer 2012.)[32] According to editor, Tom Jackson, the artist(s) were anonymous due to possible repercussions. The designers, prisoners at Joyceville, had made the logo as part of the 2010 memorial t-shirts. These were ordered (up to 400, according to media reports), delivered and worn that day by at least 150 prisoners, but then the shirts were banned and were either confiscated, or were put into storage, as prisoners were no longer allowed to wear them.

> About a week before the T-shirts were declared contraband, [Conservative Vic] Toews, in his capacity as public safety minister, described their display as offensive and dishonourable and said he would direct the Correctional Service of Canada to ensure there were no repeat incidents.[33]

---

[30] Excerpt from "Prisoner's Justice Day" by Peter M. Collins (*#079283B* published July 2011: http://joanr73.wordpress.com/2011/07/07/prisoners-justice-day-by-pete-collins/)

[31] As published in *The Peak*, Vol 51, Issue 7, August 8, 2012. "Prisoner Justice Day: A Brief history of How it Started" Compiled by Bryan Hill. http://guelphpeak.org/vol51/2012/08/prisoner-justice-day-a-brief-history-of-how-it-started/

[32] *Cell Count* (Issue 66, Summer 2012). Published by PASAN (a community-based organization to provide "advocacy, education and support to prisoners and youth in custody on HIV/AIDS and related issues". http://www.pasan.org/Cell_Count/Cell_Count_-_Issue_66.pdf

[33] Yanagisawa, Sue. "Inmates' lawsuit over T-shirts not over: lawyer", *Kingston Whig-Standard*, Thursday, May 29, 2014. http://www.thewhig.com/2014/05/29/inmates-lawsuit-over-t-shirts-not-over-lawyer

ARTS: PRISONER'S JUSTICE DAY 135

With the help of lawyers Shane Martinez and Davin Charney, those 150 prisoners filed a class action lawsuit in 2012 "to teach the state 'not to engage in actions that infringe people's charter rights.'"[34] [Sailors at sea recognize the upside down flag as a sign of distress.]

> "The T-shirts, according to Martinez, were meant to express a message to those in power," that "Canada is really in a state of social and political distress," with respect to justice issues.

---

[34] *Ibid.*

Free speech, he maintained, is uniquely valued among those "marginalized and isolated from society."[35]

Then in Issue #67[36] of *Cell Count* ran the editor's note:

"The 'Summer Issue-#66' of Cell Count was banned from 10 buckets/joints in Canada. 'Public Health Info' & 'Freedom of Speech' are still: 'Not Allowed in Canada'!"

The lawsuit was set aside in 2014, but the many battles over free speech and free expression by prisoners continue.

CANADIAN PRISONS ARE HOME TO:

Over-Incarceration of Indigenous People and People from Racialized Communities * Harsh Sentences for Non-Violent Crimes * Classism * Lack of Harm Reduction Policies and Programs * Personality Assassination * Coercive Behavioural Modification * Oppression * Racism * Fear * Double/Triple Bunking * High Rates of Infectious Diseases * Over-Incarceration of People with Mental Health Issues * Higher Security Classification of Indigenous Women * Inadequate Educational Opportunities * Transphobia * Substandard Health Care * Homophobia * Stigma and Discrimination * Persecution of Visiting Families and Friends * Human Rights Violations * Non-Conformity to United Nations Minimum Standards for the Treatment of Prisoners * Inadequate Opportunities for Personal Growth * Segregation and Isolation * Inadequate Release Support * Arbitrary Punishment * Abuse of Power * Hopelessness *

Till the walls fall, the bars bend, the chains rust and the locks break, we will remember.

By Peter M. Collins #079283B [in 2008]

---

[35] *Ibid.*

[36] Jackson, Tom. "Editor's Note" *Cell Count,* #67, Fall 2012, pg.4 http://www.pasan.org/Cell_Count/Cell_Count_-_Issue_67.pdf

Many say the observance of the day through hunger and work strikes has been lessening inside prisons in the past decade, as the action around PJD has grown into a routine. But this tension between keeping one's head down, and standing up to remember the importance of past struggles has always been part of it, too:

From 1986:

> "In an interview for Kent Times with Jack McCann and Bobby Paul on PJD, Steve Reid provides a sense of the meaning of those past struggles and their accomplishments.
>
> KT: As a survivor of long years in solitary as chronicled in Prisoners of Isolation how do you look back on those times of heavy prison-prisoner confrontations?
>
> JM: Guys don't realize the fury, the anger, the bitterness. The pain that a lot of guys put out to achieve some change. I mean we were hurt. We were hurt.
>
> KT: So August 10th symbolizes the cost of achieving change?
>
> JM: Exactly. I remember the cost.
>
> BP: The hole. There's a good example right there. Now you can smoke. You get your meals. Look how many years were spent on bread and water. Not too long ago neither. That's something that came about because of the guys who were sacrificed. The guys who died, the other guys who spent years in solitary being labelled ringleaders. The younger guys don't realize it, they [the Canadian Penitentiary Service] or nobody didn't just come along and say "hey, we better change this." It was changed because it was brought to people's attention with blood, literally with blood. Then they changed it (Kent Times, 1986:17).[37]

---

[37] Gaucher, Robert. "Organizing Inside: Prison Justice Day (August 10th) A Non-Violent Response to Penal Repression" in the *Journal of Prisoners on Prisons*, Vol. 3 Number 1 & 2 Autumn, 1990/ Spring, 1991: Capital Punishment & Prison Justice Day

As Clare Culhane put it, in her third book on prisons *"No Longer Barred from Prison: Social Injustice in Canada"*[38]:

> We can only proceed, individually and collectively, to make whatever improvements are possible in our respective areas of concern, sustained by the hope that others are doing the same.

PRISON JUSTICE DAY

WORD IS OUT BENEFIT
FRIDAY AUGUST 7TH 7:00 PM
Rhizome Café, 317 East Broadway @ Kingsway
Sliding scale $10-15. Proceeds will support *The Word Is Out*, a women in prison news service.

MUSIC LOUD
READINGS Lora McElhinney & Anne Stone
FILM SCREENING Prison Town USA
COAST SALISH WELCOME Cease Wyss

MEMORIAL RALLY
MONDAY AUGUST 10TH 6:00 PM
Claire Culhane Memorial Bench, Trout Lake Park, East Vancouver, SE corner of the lake, near the snack bar and large playground. Rain or shine.

SPEAKERS will include ex-prisoners and prisoners' rights activists.

National Prison Justice day was started in 1975 by prisoners in canada to remember all the men and women who have died unnatural deaths inside prison. On August 10th prisoners across the country go on a work stoppage and refuse to eat. On the outside it is a day to build solidarity and support for prisoners' rights issues. Visit **www.prisonjustice.ca** or the PJD table at Under the Volcano to learn more about the **cancelation of the Mother & Child Program at Alouette Correctional Centre for Women** and what you can do to support the women inside.

▲Vancouver PJD poster, 2009 [Artist: Tania Willard, 2008]
{Note the support for the Mother & Child Program at Alouette}

---

[38] Culhane, Clare. 1991. *No Longer Barred from Prison: Social Injustice in Canada.* Montreal: Black Rose Books

Two Man Cell (Peter Collins, 2005)

INTERNATIONAL DAY OF SOLIDARITY WITH PRISONERS

In 1983, prisoners in France refused to eat in recognition of August 10th, the following statement would be read on the Paris radio station Frequence-Libre:

> Why not have on August 10 an international day of solidarity with our imprisoned brothers and sisters,
> For here or elsewhere, prison kills,
> Whether it be Nalon in Ontario, Bader or Meinhoff in West Germany,
> Claude or Ivan in Switzerland, Bobby Sands in Ireland,
> Mirval, Haadjadj, Onno, Youssef or so many others in France,
> Whether they are serving 53 years like Alexandre Cotte or 16 years like Youssef,
> Whether they are considered political or common prisoners,
> PRISON KILLS!

By the mid 1990's prisoners in parts of Germany, England and the United States would join this day of peaceful protest.

INSIDE /OUTSIDE SUPPORT:
"ALL PRISONERS ARE POLITICAL PRISONERS"

Outside the prison walls, people still gather for vigils, demonstrations, "noise rallies" (so they can be heard inside), or they gather at places of significance to the struggle. There are 'Books to Prisoners' & postcard mailings meetings, lots of different campus and community radio station programming, various documentaries shown, film nights, art shows & fundraisers held, all sorts of ways of gathering to remind each other and to bring the noise out to the public attention. The stories of those who have been lost are often told and retold in these gatherings, their names remembered, and their humanity raised up.

▲ Rocky Dobey "Prison Justice Day: August 10 is Prison Justice Day. PJD started in Canada in 1976 to pay tribute to prisoners who died in prison. On this day, prisoners hold a work stoppage while outside activists organize public events."
This is a striking 2 color offset printed poster (11"x17") which was unsigned/unlimited edition [Year?]; part of the "Celebrate People's History" Series ($4 via http://www.justseeds.org/celebrate_peoples_history/02prisonjust.html)

ARTS: PRISONER'S JUSTICE DAY 141

In Vancouver, a memorial gathering has often been held at the Clare Culhane Memorial Bench in Trout Lake Park. She was a long-time prison justice activist of great courage and determination, who passed away in 1996.

Her contributions to the movement are often remembered along with other histories of the day.

▶ Photo Date? By:?
www.prisonjustice.ca/action/claire_culhane.html

▶ Another image from Rocky, this one features prominently the 13½ —a common recurring symbol of prisoner defiance in the face of bad odds: "12 jurors, 1 judge, and ½ a chance."

At Collins Bay in Kingston, Ontario, in 2012, there was a demonstration against prison expansion.

◀ Aug, 2012. "Help Stop All Construction at Collin's Bay Institution" | [Artist: ?]
more @ **endthepic.wordpress.com**[39]

---

[39] http://prisonstatecanada.blogspot.ca/2012/07/prisoner-justice-day-august-10-2012.html

In Montreal that same year, people took it right to the doorstep of the coroner, calling out for justice:

> Every year people die in prison, murdered by a system that refuses them adequate care, puts them in situations of abuse, subjects them to violence, is designed to rob them of their humanity. August 10 is a day in which we remember those who have died on the inside, and demand an end to the travesty that is the prison system. Join us for a vigil in front of the offices of the coroner, whose job it is to cover up deaths on the inside.[40]

According to Megan Kinch, in *The Dominion*, actions were also taken in Toronto and Hamilton that year:[41]

> On August 10, 2012 in Toronto, about 100 people gathered outside The Don Jail (formally The Toronto Jail, a provincial prison) to read a statement that had been written by prisoners themselves. Many in the crowd were directly affected by the prison system through their own personal encounters or through the imprisonment of those they cared about.

> Last Friday in Hamilton 50 protesters marched against lockdowns and poor conditions[42] at the Barton Street Jail (formally the Hamilton Wentworth Detention Centre) as a result of a work-to-rule action on the part of the guards. Just this week, early the morning of Wednesday September 12, only hours after correctional officers returned to work, a 42-year-old inmate was found dead.

In such conditions, simply communicating about conditions on the inside to people on the outside becomes a form or resistance.

---

[40] *Ibid*. "Vigil, Testimonies, Audio Documentaries, and Commemoration in memory of those who died in custody August 10, 2012 from 2-4pm 1701 Parthenais Street [Montreal], outside the Coroner's office

[41] Kinch, Megan. "Reporting as Resistance: Prisoner: Prisoners shed light on conditions by blogging from the inside". *The Dominion*, Sept. 17, 2005. http://www.dominionpaper.ca/articles/4623

[42] K., Devin. "Solidarity with prisoners, not OPSEU 248" Aug. 22, 2012. in *Linchpin*: http://linchpin.ca/content/Work-workplace/Solidarity-prisoners-not-OPSEU-248

▶ "Candle" by Peter Collins. Of it, he says,

> "I did this design for the 2003 August 10th memorial. The design was censored by the Administration for being offensive to the CSC. Apparently, they feel it shows them in a bad light!?"

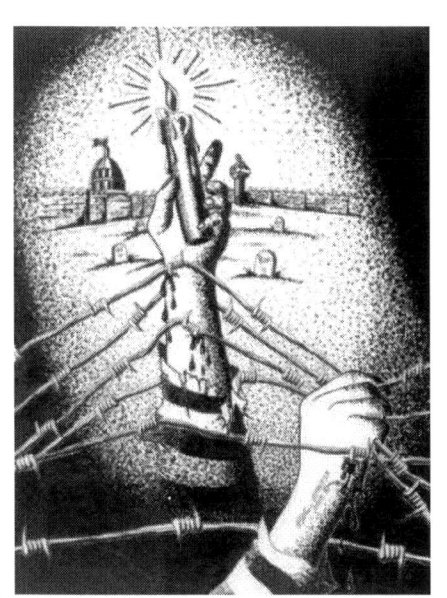

▶ This image also via "La Journée pour les Droits des PrisonnierEs Montréal & QPIRG Concordia" and it appeared also in a report from 2003 out of Australia, where a group of folks with Justice Action and Prisoner's Action Group (and others) wanted to observe the annual "IPJD" (International Prisoner Justice Day) and formed a small solidarity brigade on August 10 to go to Silverwater Jail Complex. They reported things went smoothly that day with "no tensions at all", visiting (listening & speaking with family members and friends in the visitor's room, and also using megaphones so that they could be heard on the inside) and sharing copies of their magazine. But they add that it wasn't always so:

> in 1997 a JA group celebrating the day, handing out balloons and gifts to visitors entering Silverwater were assaulted by prison officers. The officers had two dogs, almost pushed over a man with a 20 month baby and strangled a 17 year old woman with a camera strap. Police refused to charge the officers. However the next year an even larger support group was permitted to remain there without interference. It has been celebrated each year. (2003, 8)[43]

---

[43] "International Prisoners Justice Day 2003". in *Framed: The Magazine of Justice Action* (Issue 45), October 2003.

*Some of the issues addressed by
Prisoner's Justice Day over the years....*

Double Bunking
Youth Incarceration
Safe Tattooing Inside
Special Handling Units
The Wrongfully Convicted
Twenty-five Year Sentences
The Right to Freedom of Speech
The Women Self-defense Review
Abolition of National Parole Board
The Right to Vote in Federal Elections
Decriminalization of Victimless Crime
Health Care Needs of Prisoners With HIV & AIDS
Return to Shorter Sentences with 1/3 Time Off For Good Behaviour
Medical Care & Same Options for Treatment as Outside Prison
Integration of Protective Custody prisoners into General Population
Decarceration—Release Prisoners Who Already Served The Sentence
Alternatives to Incarceration - the Eventual Abolition of Prisons
The Recognition of Political Prisoners in Canada
Early Intervention Programs for At-Risk Youth
Moratorium on the Building of New Prisons
The Incarceration of Refugee Claimants
The Prisoners´ Right to Unionize
Privatization of Food Services
Needle Exchange Programs
Privatization of Prisons
Involuntary Transfers
Education Programs
Gating of Prisoners

[these words & design, with more background
on Prisoner's Justice Day, *via http://prisonjustice.ca*
who say it's based on notes published by the
Vancouver Prison Justice Day Committee in 2001]

PRISONJUSTICE.CA

via the **End Immigration Detention Network**[44]:
In support of 191 migrants on strike in Lindsay, ON
#MigrantStrike (began on September 17, 2013 >>
▼Artist: Tings Chak & the Public Studio [2014]

> WE ARE WIVES
> AND PARTNERS
> WHOSE CHILDREN
> LOOK AT THEIR
> FATHER'S SHOES
> AND ASK US...
> "When will they return?"

END IMMIGRATION DETENTION.COM

"Over the last year, despite being locked in cages, their resistance has continued.[45] They have boycotted their detention reviews, refused to go on lock down, and refused unjust prison orders. As a result, strike leaders have been deported, faced coercion and fines while some have been released. They continue."

"THESE WALLS WILL FALL"

This fall there will be a number of actions and concert events to mark the one year anniversary.
More info @ their website: endimmigrationdetention.com or (705)340-4432 or migrantstrike @gmail.com

---

[44] http://endimmigrationdetention.com/

[45] http://guelphpeak.org/news-updates/2014/07/end-immigration-detention/

ART and/in MIGRANT DETENTION prisoner justice day: aug 10, 6-8pm

▲ Via Tings Chak and The Public Studio... Aug.10, 2014

"TODAY, Prisoners' Justice Day. And in the spirit of this day, which began as an act of mass civil disobedience nearly 40 years ago at Millhaven, we remember and honour those who have lived, resisted, and lost their lived in prison. The 15,000 across Canada, occupied Turtle island in federal penitentiaries, the thousands more in provincial prisons, on remand, and under state supervision, and the hundreds of migrant women, men, and children locked up in prisons and detention centres right now.

"In resisting the prison industrial complex, we must recognize who this system criminalizes and violently targets: Indigenous, poor, and racialized people, migrants, sex-workers, and drug-using people, disabled, queer/trans/gender non-conforming folks.

"Prisons force us to connect our struggles. And today we honour and remember the nearly 2000 people killed in Gaza. This occupation traumatically reveals how the violence of borders and violence of occupation and de facto imprisonment are part of one struggle—that the fight for the freedom to move in search of flourishing lives, the freedom to stay and resist displacement, and the freedom to return to the places we call home means that we must tear all the fences down ... that anti-borders work is anti-prison work." [46]

Finally, the words of prisoners at Drumheller in 2009, impress the importance of immediate action; after a long description of how rotten prisons were in the 1970's, and how much has been won, they note the decline of these gains in the past decade:

> But guess what--every year we lose some of these things. One by one they are slowly being taken away and there seems to be no end in sight. Even Healthcare services are

---

[46] Tings Chak > "AUG 10: Prisoners' Justice Day: ART and/in MIGRANT DETENTION", a public event in Toronto, "honouring creative resistance in immigration detention through conversation, screen-printing and letter-writing." https://www.facebook.com/events/621525571279487/

being scaled back, the increasing costs touted as the rationale, but how many times have guys heard the "we can only give you what someone on welfare would get" reasoning when denied a type of medication or treatment? The availability and frequency of pre-release passes into the community are also being gradually reduced--they say due to media and CSC corporate image concerns.

Well, regardless of the reasons, or what particular this or that we have or had, the bottom line and indisputable fact is that us prisoners have less now than we did ten years ago. Want to guess how much we will have ten years from now--more or less? Think about how much we are going to lose in the ten years after that. So, please do not forget those who came before us and what they fought for, because there will come a day not far from now when prisoners like you and me wake up and realize we've lost all of what we once had, and then we will have stand together and fight to get it back.[47]

This retrospective was compiled in anticipation of the upcoming 40th anniversary of that first strike at Millhaven, and it is by no means a comprehensive survey of all the Prisoners Justice Day related artworks, in fact there are many more significant pieces that we could not include at this time. However, we would like to contribute to the archiving and cataloging of these important visual histories, as well as strengthen the networks of those who continue to remember and resist, and we will definitely publish more abolitionist art in upcoming issues.

We are especially interested in oral, written and/or sketched histories & herstories of the movements against prison injustice (not only under/across the Canadian state). If you know of some work(s) that we've omitted, or there is something new or original which you'd like to see included in a future publication,

please get in touch with us at
editors@radicalcriminology.org

---

[47] "Prisoner's Justice Day" by OBM staff & Co. in *The Drum: The Drumheller Newsletter* (#18, August 2009, pages 6-7) http://penalpress.com/wp-content/uploads/DrumAugust2009.pdf

Seeking Justice for Missing and Murdered Native Women

LISA MONCHALIN

I present to you one woman's testament
About acknowledging a crisis where 824 is the new estimate

What is this number you might ask?
It's the number of missing and murdered Native women
the government tries to mask

For some this might be a shock
For others it's an everyday walk

Families mourning the ones who have passed
Others hoping the last time they saw them wasn't their last

Some might have heard of the diseased pig farmer whose name does not merit mention
Yes, for many Native peoples this brings about a discomforting tension

So please remember the names of the valued women who the media insufficiently cover

Such as Brenda Wolfe a wonderful and strong Aboriginal women and mother

Or Georgina Papin who loved her culture and was great at baking
And moccasins and dream catchers you could find her making

Or Sherry Irving who was known for her love of rock music and having fun
And whose heart so beautiful she sparkled like the sun

Or Tanya Marlo Holyk who liked basketball, and other sports
And who loved to read and enjoyed doing book reports

Or Mona Wilson the youngest of five and so very smart
And as her brother explained—she had a true love in her heart

Or Dawn Crey who loved her son so much
Whose braveness and strength—and many hearts she did touch

These are real women whose stories are not always told
Do not buy into what the media might have sold

These women are mothers, daughters, sisters, friends, and wives
People who are beautiful and deserve to live out their full lives

Violence affects our women disturbingly way to much

More likely to be stalked, raped, and unwantedly touched

Seven times more likely to become homicide prey
And much more likely to be violated against our will in some way
Three times more likely to be killed by a stranger
Yes, for Native women this exists as a true danger

We are three times more likely to become a victim of a violent crime
But let me tell you—this is not reflective of traditional time

Violence against our women was never traditional
In fact, our women were leaders in what is medicinal

Before the wrath of colonization hit
We had central roles, and on our traditional councils we would sit

Women across Turtle Island had many talents
We made major decisions and lived in balance

But it doesn't stop there
All Native peoples have an inner drive to care

Yet Patriarchy came in like a violence disease
As soon as those deeply sick people crossed those seas

It happened right from the start
All of the explorers played a part
They arrived with an ingrained notion of superiority

Then set out to make Native peoples a minority

They did it by disease and direct killing
Then surveyed our land for the tilling

Miguel Cuneo accompanied Columbus on his second trip across the sea
Some of you might wonder—well who is he?

Well Columbus "gifted" him with a Native woman to whom he had lust
Telling him he could do whatever he must

Cuneao in his own words said he had thrashed and forced rape
And found humour in her trying to escape

And what is it hidden behind a rhetoric of excuses?
It is these people who are held as heroes—ones who have committed atrocious abuses

They claimed land that wasn't for sale
They ripped through our communities honoring the white violent male

In the name of the church the children they did steal
Forcing them into residential schools where they would struggle to get a decent meal

Children taken right from the hands of mom and dad
Where hair was cut and they destroyed anything they had
Abuses against children reached epidemic heights

With priests and administrators who went lurking in the nights

Although the doors of the schools are now shut
The legacy of trauma continues like an open cut

Genocidal policies and laws such as the Indian Act
Make it seem like governments have formed some sick pact

Enough putting up with the government's ridiculous shit
Like Idle No more proclaimed we are no longer going to be on the couch and sit

The Mohawks at Tyendinaga have been protesting for an inquiry
Demanding justice and truth to be spoken in its entirety

And although you might think this does not affect you in a direct way
Remember we are all related—so what role are you willing to play?

Attend a vigil or say a prayer
But please, don't just walk away or simply stare

Remember all these are our sisters and it's not too late
Such as Maisy and Shannon who having been missing since 2008

Maisy Odijick is known for being helpful and sharing
And like her aunty Maria explained—she is very caring

Shannon Alexander—kindhearted and strong
But these two girls having been missing for way too long

Gone missing without a trace
And yet it took two weeks for the media to even cover their case

Families and parents struggling to get support from the police
Maisy's Aunty Maria—started a website to find her niece

And for those who choose to turn a blind eye
What is it you tell yourself—some kind of lie?

For those that argue stories are too hard to hear?
I say, try living every day in pain and fear

I challenge you to put yourself in another's shoes
Such as one of these women's kids or moms—what do you have to lose?

Perhaps your own privilege you might have to face
Yes, this might be the case

But please don't shy away
Take a stand, join and stay

Raise awareness—and justice please demand
Let everyone know in your own way—you are taking a stand
And although the government is still replying with shuns
Remember beautiful women—we miss you tons

[insurgencies]

Anarchism: A critical analysis.

CHRIS HOWELL[1]

Anarchism is a radical social-political theory that aims to deconstruct the State in order to empower every one; empower by granting liberty and equality. An old saying of Bakunin is paraphrased, "equality without liberty is tyranny, liberty without equality is gross injustice" (Shantz, 2013). Anarchism asserts that in order to grant liberty to all and treat all as equals, we must abolish the authoritarian state. So, the three, interconnected ideals discussed here are foundational to anarchism: 1) abolishing the authoritarian state; 2) liberty; and 3) equality. After examining the interrelations of the three key ideals, I shall focus on one criticism surrounding human nature.

Of course, there are more than a few conceptualizations of anarchism, however the tradition I focus on here is communal anarchism—as opposed to individualized anarchism or other forms—as conceptualized by Peter Kropotkin and others (Guerin, 2005, Kropotkin, 2009, & Chomsky, 2005), which relies on cooperation and compassion (Kropotkin, 2009).

As can be seen in Canada and other capitalist societies, capitalism is structured in a manner that benefits the few at the cost of the many, communism is the opposite, it is structured in a

---

[1] Chris Howell wrote this as an undergrad student at Kwantlen Polytechnic University in Surrey, and he was a co-organizer (with the Critical Criminology Working Group) of the North American Anarchist Studies Network's 5th Annual Conference in January 2014 at Kwantlen. He is now doing his MA graduate studies at Carleton University in Ottawa.

manner that benefits the many at the cost of the few (Kropotkin, 2005 as presented by Guerin). According to anarchism, in both cases the State—whether representing one, few or many—through the rule of law and the criminal justice system, imposes their will onto others by force (Russell, 1966). In its purest sense, anarchism aims to give the power back to the people; all people; equally. From my understanding, anarchism rejects both models by arguing no authoritarian state should be in control, thus empowering everyone through liberty and equality, not merely transferring power from one group to another nor merely relying on economic equality.

ABOLISH THE AUTHORITARIAN STATE

To abolish the authoritarian state means there should not be an external power that creates, imposes, and/or enforces rules on others (Chomsky, 2005, Guerin, 2005, Kropotkin, 2009, & Russell, 1966). In other words, anarchism argues we must remove the forcible government as seen in capitalist, communist, dictatorships and so forth. The authoritarian state has control of the rules society must abide by and the State is granted the power to enforce these rules. This inherently grants them power of our freedoms. Look at Canada for example, the Canadian Criminal Code controls what all persons in Canada cannot do, the Canadian Charter of Fundamental Rights and Freedoms controls which freedoms are upheld, and the Canadian Criminal Justice system enforces those rules. Thus, the Canadian State controls, legally speaking, what we can and cannot do, thus it sets the parameters of *our freedoms*.

Noam Chomsky argues, in reference to all forms of authority that include the State, that we must challenge all authority and place the burden of proof on the authority to justify their legitimacy in restricting our freedoms. From this it can be inferred that anarchists place a high burden of proof on the authoritarian state but a necessary one. Meaning, if we grant the Canadian government the power to control its citizens (and visitors) then they must justify their actions, since in order to grant the State this power, we must lose freedoms. You cannot have absolute freedoms and external force that controls your actions. Anarchism asserts that there is no sufficient justification for giving up any freedoms; hence we must abolish all authoritarian control.

LIBERTY

Liberty, as defined by Thomas Hobbes, a social contract philosopher, is "the absence of Opposition; (by Opposition I mean external Impediments of motion) and may be applied no lesse to Irrational, and Inanimate creatures, than to Rationall [sic]" (Hobbes, 2007, p. 94). J.S. Mill, a pioneer utilitarian philosopher, argues persons ought to be free—thought, speech, and action—as long as their actions do not harm others (harm principle) (Mill, 2011). In sum, these definitions define liberty as individual freedoms of thought and action, not controlled by an external force (state control) rather controlled by the individual. The first two definitions are by philosophers whom conceptualize the term, but are both promoters of the social contract and state control (although state control in a more limited manner than the current Canadian model). However, the problem with these philosophers' approaches are that they believe state control is necessary in granting and enforcing liberty. As argued earlier, if the state or any external force controls liberties then it undermines the definition of liberty; absolute freedoms.

Anarchists argue for the same ideal; absolute individual freedoms or liberty, but disregard the notion that persons need a social contract held by an external power (typically state control) controlling, in essence, their lives and definitely controlling their freedoms. Michael Bakunin (2005) states,

> ... liberty that consists in the full development of all of the material, intellectual and moral powers that latent in each person; liberty that recognizes no restrictions other than those determined by the laws of our own individual nature, which cannot properly be regarded as restrictions since these laws are not imposed by any outside legislator beside or above us, but are immanent and inherent, forming the very basis of our material, intellectual and moral being —they do not limit us but are the real and immediate conditions of our freedom (As quoted by Chomsky, p. 122).

In this case Bakunin, an anarchist, argues that if we are to be truly free agents (absolute freedom), then we ought to be restricted only by our own individual nature and our own moral code, not by state controlled freedoms. Only then can 'absolute freedoms' be given their name, not when an external force deems it with limitations.

MUTUAL AID

In order to obtain absolute freedoms, we must abolish state control and uphold true individual autonomy of rights. Kropotkin argues, and I agree, that in order for absolute liberty to flourish, we must work together in a cooperative and compassionate manner (Kropotkin, 2009). Since, persons are generally good (Marxist/Anarchist belief), if liberty flourishes then human beings will progress in a positive manner as a community.

Mutual aid is conceptualized as the state of human nature that persons are protective, equal and supportive of one another (Kropotkin, 2009). Notably, that does not mean that human nature cannot also be selfish, it merely means that under the appropriate structure human beings are capable of cooperating. In other words it is natural for persons to be both selfish and cooperative. Kropotkin comes to his conclusion of human nature by analyzing the historical evolution of humankind; social Darwinism. As Kropotkin (2009) states,

> It is evident that it would be quite contrary to all that we know of [human] nature if men were an exception to general a rule: if a creature so defenceless [sic] as man was at his beginning should have found his protective and his way to progress, not in mutual support; like other animals, but in reckless [sic] competition for personal advantages with no regard to the interests of the species (p. 74).

Kropotkin uses the early stages of humanity to support, effectively, the notion that history proves that we can work cooperatively and compassionately without state control, otherwise we would not have survived.

Kropotkin argues that human beings evolved from band-based animals, which are meant for group settings not intended for individual settings nor small group (family/communal) settings as representative of our current model (Kropotkin, 2009). "Zoology and palaeo-ethnology are thus agreed in considering that the band, not the family, was the earliest form of social life" (Kropotkin, 2009, p. 149). The evolutionary history supports that human beings not only can work together in a cooperative and compassionate manner (mutual aid) but they can progress as a species more effectively.

In extension, Kinna (2005) writes, "On the contrary, the abolition of the state will put an end to violence and repression and herald a new—more harmonious—social order. Moreover, it will release individuals from constraints of authority and enable them to enjoy their freedom" (p. 76). "[Mutual aid] is that individuals are legitimately shaped by the moral, social and cultural mores of their communities . . . the making of that "whole" we call a rounded, creative, and richly variegated human being crucially depends upon community supports" (Kinna, 2005, p. 76). Kinna's quote shows the dependency and interconnection between equality/mutual aid, absolute freedoms, and the abolition of the State. Mutual aid helps connect individuals through bonds; liberty flourishes through mutual aid; mutual aid and liberty are only possible through abolishing the authoritarian state. Through a process of breaking state interference, and building greater horizontal community connections and support networks, persons value themselves and others more; these are common principles of anarchism.

CRITIQUE OF ANARCHISM

A criticism of anarchism focuses on human nature, criticizing the belief that people are capable of being cooperative and compassionate if there is no external authoritarian force. In order to thoroughly look at the criticism presented, I look to G.A. Cohen and Bertrand Russell, whom are both philosophers that advocate for socialism but use differing arguments. Cohen in "Why not Socialism", argues for a communal socialism (which is not anarchism), however his argument applies to anarchism. Cohen provides a construction of the criticism and a rebuttal to the criticism. On the other hand, I look to Russell in "Roads to Freedom", whom provides a legitimate account to anarchism (as well as socialism and syndicalism), then critically analyzes the theory. Both these philosophers argue for a socialist state that would have an authoritarian state in control which is inconsistent with anarchism but their arguments help understand a criticism of anarchism. The criticism is that human nature is not cooperative and compassionate, or at least not cooperative and compassionate enough for an anarchist society to work.

The criticism that Cohen and Russell present is that persons are not generally good (cooperative and compassionate), rather they are egoists (Cohen, 2009 & Russell, 1966). If persons are egoists then people will not work well together on their own, humanity will not positively progress, therefore we need a social contract in order to work together in a manner that all persons may work well together; a simplified version of a commonly accepted argument for a state-controlled social contract (Cohen, 2009). The initial conflict lies with assumptions of human nature; egoism versus mutual aid. Hobbes goes on to argue that the state of nature is a "war of each against all", which is a form of extreme competition (Kropotkin, 2009, p. 75 as Kropotkin displays Hobbes' argument). If human nature is an extreme competition between individuals, then anarchism will not work, since people will do whatever it takes to personally gain, even if that causes harm to others.

According to this criticism, the only way for persons to work well with others is if there is a ruler that will impose, enforce, and control us in a manner that is conducive to us cooperating with one another. Without the State, we will naturally return to our selfish actions, thus be unable to cooperate in a manner that is needed for anarchism to work as a communal and/or societal structure. Thus Russell asserts anarchism cannot be designed in a manner that will force us to work against our human nature (Cohen, 2009).

Cohen provides an example to help refute the claim that we are egoists; the hypothetical camping trip. In brief, the hypothetical camping trip refers to a group of people that cooperate together in order to collectively provide food, shelter, preparation, cooking, cleaning, and supplies among other means that individuals may work collectively (Cohen, 2009). There is no hierarchy that separates individuals within the group and the group works cohesively to provide sufficient supplies for everyone, but enables different persons to provide different help, according to their skills and interests (Cohen, 2009). For example, imagine that you are an excellent hunter but hate cooking and cleaning, while I prefer cooking and cleaning. In this example we would work together so that you supply and prepare the food, and I cook the food and clean the mess afterwards. An oversimplification of the camping trip, but the point is to show that there are a group of various people with differing interests and skills, like in society, that are capable of working well together in a cooperative manner that benefits everyone.

Now, one could criticize the hypothetical camping trip by arguing that it does not truly represent a larger community or society. Merely because it is imaginable or practical for a camping trip does not mean it will work for a larger, more complicated group. To which, Cohen states that there are cases in which the camping trip work for a larger community; merely look to any emergency situation (Cohen, 2009, p. 54). Take the flood in Calgary, Alberta that happened in 2013, and that caused immense damage to communities in the area. After the flood, rather than selfishly work for one's own needs and desires, individuals from the local communities (and beyond) worked together to provide care, support and compassion to affected members of the community (McMurray & Sun, 2013). If we are merely egoists as Hobbes and Russell believe, then why were so many people willing to help Calgary flood victims? I believe, as Cohen exemplifies, that we are capable of cooperating and compassion, but it is the societal structure (capitalism) that conditions and/or promotes us into being egoists.

Although Cohen's example of the emergency situations extends to a larger community unlike in the hypothetical camping trip, there remains a concern of generality; can emergency situations indicate the same response as in everyday life? I believe Cohen successfully shows that we are capable of cooperation and compassion, thus not merely egoists, but are we naturally or can we be sufficiently cooperative and compassionate to remove all authoritative power?

Bertrand Russell argues no. Russell states that if every one is given absolute freedoms without external forces given control, then "the strong would oppress the weak, or the majority would oppress the minority, or the lovers of violence would oppress the more peaceable people" (Russell, 1966, p. 82). Russell's argument is that if we are given absolute freedoms, then one may act according to whim, since there would be no deterrent or power enforcing one's will. Let us take an extreme example of a sociopath or psychopath such as Robert Pickton. Pickton murdered numerous women largely from the downtown eastside of Vancouver, B.C. and was convicted in 2007

(Cameron, 2011). According to Russell, if people like Pickton lived in an anarchist society, then there could not be legal ramifications or imprisonment since that would restrict Pickton's freedoms and impose the will of others onto Pickton. Although likely a small number of people there will be people with violent impulses. In which case in order to be consistent with anarchism either we must grant everyone the ability to act on whim —even if they bring harm to others—in accordance with absolute freedoms, or we must have a force that reacts to innately wrong actions such as violence (Russell, 1966). Russell states, "The conclusion which appears to be forced upon us is that the Anarchist ideal of a community in which no acts are forbidden by law is not, at any rate for the present, compatible with the stability of such a world as the anarchists desire" (Russell, 1966, p. 87). This objection to anarchism does not argue that all are merely egoists, rather in a mixed group of individuals, there will be people that do not always act compassionately or cooperatively, people such as Robert Pickton or other violent offenders.

We could try to refer to the previous rebuttal again as a response to Russell's criticism, saying that capitalism produces these persons that act innately wrong. Once we restructure society in accordance with anarchist ideals, then people like Pickton will cease to exist. However, I do not believe that anyone (including an anarchist) would argue that all violence and wrongdoing would cease to exist in any society. Notably, it is conceivable that crime and egoist tendencies would be significantly lower in an anarchist society, which Russell asserts himself (Russell, 1966).

A more plausible response to Russell's criticism is to argue that he presents a false dilemma. That is in order to be consistent with anarchist ideals, if an individual commits a violent act, an anarchist must either accept the act as the individual using their freedom, or be inconsistent with their ideals and restrict the individual's freedoms in order to prevent further actions.

It seems that Russell argues that the only viable response to a crime is retribution, crime control, and/or due process models. However, there are clearly more responses to crime, such as restorative justice. Duane Ruth-Heffelbower (2011) argues that anarchism is consistent with restorative justice, since restorative justice, also, removes power from an external power and gives it to the victim, offender, and community. Restorative justice is a response to crime that effectively focuses on and discusses the victim's needs, the offender's needs and the community's needs, in a manner that does not restrict freedoms but does respond to the wrongdoing in order to 'restore' the community to how it was prior to the act (Ruth-Heffelbower, 2011). For instance, if a person struck another person, then through a restorative justice model the three parties could work together to tell their story, uncover their needs, and work together in order to come to a solution. I agree with Ruth-Heffelbower's argument that as opposed to retribution, crime control models, and due process, restorative justice is not only a possible response to crime but a more effective response in helping the collective good.

In this case, Ruth-Heffelbower (2011) provides a response to crime that seems consistent with anarchism. Perhaps Russell would respond that in order for restorative justice to be consistent with anarchism, it cannot punish or restrict any freedoms of the offender. Further, the victim and/or community could not even force the offender, victim, and/or community to participate in the restorative process, as that would be restricting on one's freedoms.

I do not have a definitive answer to Russell's criticism, there seems to be something significantly wrong with ensuring absolute freedoms to those that harm others. I feel one plausible response would be to grant absolute freedoms but if they commit a heinous act—for instance theft and violence—that restricts another person's freedoms, then the community is granted the ability to limit rights. However, this would only work if the community can agree on terms through a participatory democracy of all individuals. Meaning if an offense is agreed on by all, then all would agree on an appropriate reaction from the community.

Conclusion

There remain questions about the feasibility of anarchism in connection with human nature. On the one hand, absolute freedoms for all is desirable, which necessitates abolishing the

State, however, on the other hand, how can or how should anarchism respond to agreed upon criminal acts? Is it consistent to say that you are granted absolute freedoms until you harm others, then the community is justified in restricting your freedoms. If one is to go down that path then it seems the agreed upon "laws" would have to be very narrow, and follow J.S. Mill's "harm principle" which would mean the community only reacts to offenders, when the offender causes harm (physical or monetary) to the victim(s). It is an area that definitely brings up consistency issues, but the anarchist ideals are worth pursuing.

References

Cameron, S. (2011). *On the Farm: Robert William Pickton and the Tragic Story of Vancouver's Missing Women*. Random House LLC.

Chomsky, N. (2005). *Chomsky on Anarchism* (1st ed.). Oakland, CA: AK Press.

Cohen, G. A. (2009). *Why Not Socialism?* Princeton University Press.

Guérin, D. (2005). *No Gods, No Masters* (Complete unabridged ed.). Edinburgh, Scotland ; Oakland, CA: AK Press.

Hobbes, T. (2007). Leviathan. text. Retrieved November 7, 2013, from http://ebooks.adelaide.edu.au/h/hobbes/thomas/h68l/

Kinna, R. (2005). *Anarchism: a beginners guide*. Oxford: Oneworld.

Kropotkin, P. (2009). *Mutual Aid*. Echo Library.

McMurray, J., & Sun, C. (n.d.). Call for flood recovery volunteers sees overwhelming response at Calgary's McMahon Stadium. *Calgary Sun*. Retrieved November 1, 2013, from http://www.calgarysun.com/2013/06/24/call-for-flood-recovery-volunteers-sees-overwhelming-response-at-calgarys-mcmahon-stadium

Mill, J. S. (2011). *On Liberty*. MobileReference.

Russell, B. (1966). *Roads to freedom: socialism, anarchism and syndicalism* (3rd ed.). London: Allen & Unwin.

Ruth-Heffelbower, D. (2011). Anarchist criminology: a new way to understand a set of proven practices. Retrieved November 1, 2013 from http://peace.fresno.edu/docs/Anarchist_criminology.pdf.

Shantz, J. (2013, Fall). Contemporary Sociological Criminology [CRIM 3111 class lecture]. Richmond, Canada: Kwantlen Polytechnic University.

[book reviews]

The Struggle Within: Prisons, Political Prisoners, and Mass Movements in the United States
by Dan Berger
Forward by Ruth Wilson Gilmore,
Afterword by dream hampton

(Montreal and Oakland: Kersplebedeb and PM Press, 2014. 110 pages.)
http://danberger.org/?page_id=111

Reviewed by—Jordan House,
York University, April 2014

"More militancy!" is an oft-heard demand of the left. It is the subject of position papers and propaganda, of academic study and debate. We lament militancy of days past: the wildcat strikes, the mass demonstrations, the fighting movements. But we must not forget that the militancy of yesteryear was not without casualties. In particular, we have inherited the legacy of militants of the recent past. We have our martyrs: some, like Black Panthers George Jackson and Fred

Hampton, were killed. Many others, from a diverse range of movements, completed and continue to serve long prison sentences. Dan Berger's *The Struggle Within* is an overview of these militants and the movements from which they came.

The Struggle Within serves as an excellent primer on United States political prisoners and the relationship of various left movements to the carceral system. Despite his own claim that the book represents only an "introductory and incomplete sketch," Berger demonstrates an expansive and comprehensive knowledge of US revolutionary movements, covering the New Left, Anti-War, Anti-Imperialist, Black Power, Indigenous liberation, Chicano, Puerto Rican Independence, and Environmentalist movements. While mostly focusing on prisoners of struggles past, in particular those from the 1960s and 1970s, Berger links these to contemporary struggles in a critical chapter on the Patriot Act and repression in the post 9/11 era. This is key, since objectively weaker contemporary movements face increasingly sophisticated state repression, fortified by innovations in surveillance techniques and technologies and backed by new repressive laws.

The slim volume is made up of four chapters: North American Freedom Struggles; Anti-imperialism, Anti-authoritarianism, and Revolutionary non-violence; Earth and Animal Liberation; and Déjà Vu and the Patriot Act, covering the post 9/11 period. Berger moves through each section by chronicling the organizations and movements that produced prominent political prisoners, with special focus on those still locked up. In doing so, he attempts to illustrate the interconnections between the various individuals, organizations and movements he discusses. Some of these connections are easy to demonstrate, such as the (admittedly oftentimes troubled) affinity between white New Leftists and the Black Power movement. Other cases are less clear, although connections can still be identified. For example, Berger links militant environmentalism to the broader left through the figure of Judi Bari, a labor organizer and member of Earth First!, who was car bombed and subject to an attempted frame-up by the FBI. Overall Berger emphasizes that the common thread throughout the diverse movements covered is the experience of state violence, arguing that the "ubiquity of state repression affords an opportunity to forge solidarity between multiple revolutionary movements," while going on to note that this should not simply trump "contradictions" between and within movements (81). However, without a more robust framework expounding the character of state power, and some exploration of what it is that counts as 'our' movements (for example, the Tea Party has also faced state repression), it is unclear at times what exactly the miscellaneous movements of the book share in common.

Perhaps the most significant theoretical claim Berger argues is that mass incarceration in the US is not merely the result of the War on Drugs or premised upon a system of socio-economic repression and cleansing. He argues it is also significantly in response to political and social movements that have, at times, challenged state power. This is an interesting thesis that should be expanded upon, and raises several immediate questions. What does this mean given the current weak position of oppositional movements in relation to the state and capital? Are the institutions of state power expanding to successfully repress increasingly marginal oppositional movements? And if these movements are indeed increasingly marginal, what explains the expansion of state repression (since it cannot be said to be exerted in response to powerful social movements)? This, however, is the book at its most abstract. It also contains helpful and concrete resources. In addition to a relatively robust and thematically organized bibliography, Berger provides a glossary of on-the-ground organizational resources—a refreshing attempt to root the ideas put forward in the book in practice by providing a number of ways for readers to plug in as activists.

Like many thin volumes, the book suffers at times from its brevity. Most critically, readers would benefit from a more in-depth discussion of the categorization of 'political prisoner'. Berger rightly rejects liberal definitions of 'prisoners of conscience'—those imprisoned for their beliefs and not necessarily their actions—and asserts that the "state uses the imprisonment of political leaders and rank-and-file activists as a bludgeon against movement victories" (2). We are told that no one in a democracy is tried for his or her political beliefs, only for specific crimes. The fact that those who struggle against power structures are criminalized is erased from the discourse completely. As Berger explains, "Thus the central issue for thinking about political prisoners is not whether they 'did it' but what movements did they come from and what are the broader circumstances surrounding their arrests" (2). This however, is not fully fleshed out. While Berger asserts that "political prisoners serve collective prison time for all those who participated in the movement from which they emerged" (2), it is also true that the militant organizations from which many political prisoners came did not necessarily arise organically from mass movements, but emerged from them as splits. Berger explains that, "time after time, frustration at the limited possibilities of available (i.e., legal) remedies to such entrenched injustice led many activists to seek—and many more support—alternatives options to resistance" (3). These alternatives were some variation of armed struggle or 'armed propaganda.' Berger does acknowledge this tension to some degree: "upping the ante through militant, often clandestine, tactics was not intended to stand in for organizing a mass movement (although sectarianism and different strategic priorities have often yielded this in effect if not in intent)" (3). Just as movements can and must reject those who turn on them (such as those who turn state witness), it is also true that successful movements must be able to have principled critique of strategy and tactics of those individuals and groups that comprise them. This is an issue that those working to free political prisoners and those fighting broadly for social change will have to continue to develop.

Despite the book's title, Berger does not say much about the struggles within prisons, mentioning only briefly that political and politicized prisoners continue to contribute to political movements especially notably "through writing, mentoring younger activists, conducting peer education with other prisoners, and fighting AIDS, misogyny and homophobia" (81). This is especially unfortunate given that Berger has specifically written on the topic elsewhere. In an article entitled "Social Movements and Mass Incarceration," Berger discusses various parenting programs developed by prisoners in Virginia and New York State. He also emphasizes the critical role of political and politicized prisoners in pioneering peer-based HIV/AIDS programming early in the AIDS crisis.

> Rejecting the prevailing homophobia that led to terrible criminal neglect throughout the United States, these political prisoners saw

the leading campaigns in the gay community. The political prisoners' orientation towards grassroots organizing and bottom-up mobilization fit perfectly with the *peer* education and support method, later proven to be the only effective approach among prisoners. (2013, 11)

Likewise one could add the struggles of prisoners to better living and working conditions, from the National Prisoners Reform Association in Massachusetts, to the California Prisoners' Union or the North Carolina Labor Unions and more. This may be corrected with the publication of Berger's forthcoming book, *Captive Nation: Black Prison Organizing in the Civil Rights Era* (2014).

Overall, *The Struggle Within* is a contribution to a movement for social change that is aware of its own past and history of repression. Prisons have always been a fact of working class life, and will continue to be institutions that those who fight for a better world cannot ignore. Victims of the class struggle will continue to be locked up just as individuals, organizations, and movements will continue to fight. As Berger thoroughly proves, you can't jail an idea.

References

Berger, Dan. Forthcoming 2014. *Captive Nation: Black Prison Organizing in the Civil Rights Era*. Chapel Hill: UNC Press.

Berger, Dan. 2013. "Social Movements and Mass Incarceration," in *Souls: A Critical Journal of Black Politics, Culture, and Society*, 15:1-2, 3-18.

Berger, Dan. 2014. *The Struggle Within: Prisons, Political Prisoners, and Mass Movements in the United States*. Montreal and Oakland: Kersplebedeb and PM Press.

Killer Weed: Marijuana Grow Ops, Media, and Justice
by Dr. Susan Boyd and Dr. Connie Carter
http://www.notkillerweed.com/

(Toronto: University of Toronto Press, 2014. 304 pages.)

Reviewed by—Chuck Reasons J.D., Ph.D.
Visiting Professor, Criminology, Kwantlen Polytechnic University, May 2014

REEFER MADNESS
THIS IS YOUR BRAIN ON DRUGS
GATEWAY DRUG
DOPE FIENDS

These are just a few of the images of illegal drugs, drug users, and the effects of illegal drugs that have been around since the prohibition of certain drugs. Such images have been an integral part of the propaganda distributed by governments, law enforcement and other proponents of prohibition. Propaganda can be so effective, powerful, and persuasive that the information becomes taken for granted "common sense." When I say drugs, my students and most of the public think of illegal drugs, not our daily dose of caffeine, nicotine, alcohol or asperin. While these distinctions are pharmacologically unsound, they fit the dominant mythology that illegal drugs such as marijuana posses demon like qualities that will cause us to lie, steal, commit violence an use other illegal drugs. Unfortunately for the dominant mythology and the criminal policy it supports, the public and many persons in power realize they been conned. The dire consequences of using marijuana have been unfounded by the nearly 50% of Canadians and Americans who have used it. Sine the 1894 British Hemp Drug Commission Report, there have been reports noting the medical uses of marijuana and its relatively benign effect on people, particularly compared to alcohol and nicotine. The authors of KILLER DRUG document he history of the Canadian propaganda surrounding marijuana grow ops in order to maintain a punitive approach to this prohibited drug. Since "the king has no clothes" with regard to the propaganda regarding the presumed physical consequences of marijuana, attacking the way marijuana is grown becomes an alternative strategy. Drs. Boyd and Carter do not argue that there are no negative effects of marijuana use and growing, but that they have been entirely distorted and exaggerated by those wishing to maintain a criminal and punitive approach to this illegal drug.

The authors use the time honoured research technique of content analysis to study 15 years (1995-2009) of newspaper articles, pictures and headlines to determine how the image of grow ops has been "framed". The newspapers included the Vancouver Sun, Province, Globe and Mail, and Times Columnist. Particular attention is given to the Vancouver area since it is known as the "pot capital of Canada." Their analysis of 2524 articles found three themes about marijuana production emerged in all papers. These were (1) it is a threat to public safety (2) it threatens otherwise safe communities and (3) it is associated with particular criminal types and organizations. While the authors note that public opinion in B.C. is in favour of decriminalization/legalization of marijuana, marijuana related charges doubled in B.C. from 2005-2011, led by the RCMP. Not surprisingly, RCMP supported research has been the basis for much of the distorted information about marijuana grow ops.

The authors note that a major supporter of getting tough on co-ops is Dr. Darryl Plecas, professor of Criminology and Criminal Justice at University of Fraser Valley who authored/co-authored several of the RCMP reports that have been used to justify harsher penalties and a get tough approach toward marijuana grow ops. In fact, he was the RCMP University Chair in Crime Reduction at Fraser Valley. Apart from the potential appearance of lack of independence/objectivity, Boyd and Carter note that these studies are not published and peer reviewed as is normal in academic research. Nonetheless, they are widely cited by law enforcement and others promoting a get tough approach as authoritative/valid evidence of the harms of grow ops. In fact Plecas himself was often cited in newspapers reaffirming the findings. But the authors of this book show that certain reports lack scientific rigor and, in fact, mislead the reader due, in part, to faulty methods of research. However, they were widely cited and acknowledge as the real facts about marijuana grow ops. These reports became the basis of a propaganda campaign against marijuana grow ops. Ironically, the RCMP funded/supported reports suggest that B.C. emulate the policy of Washington State at the time. As Washington State and Colorado were legalizing marijuana in November 2012, the Canadian Government was increasing penalties for marijuana. I know in my home county, Kittitas, law enforcement is not happy with the change, but fortunately they are not law creators, but law enforcers.

In an interesting review of international literature on marijuana grow ops, the authors contrast the scholarly research with the slanted view of the RCMP supported research. Fortunately for Boyd and Carter, they were able to obtain a copy of a 2011 Canada Justice Report which provides refutation to many of the distortions presented in RCMP related research and pronouncements. The report was not released by the government, but obtained through an Access to Information Act request. For example, the RCMP, among others, assert that grow ops are largely run by organized crime, but only 5% of offenders in court cases concerning grow ops were affiliated with organized crime, according to the Justice study. Contrary to the racialized image of grow ops Boyd and Carter found in the media, the Justice study found most were white and 94% were Canadian citizens.

In terms of the image of marijuana and grow ops being frequent sources of violence, the authors note that the use of marijuana does not produce violence. Most violence associated with illegal drugs, including marijuana, is a consequence of the drug being illegal and market/territory issues. The tragic case of the Surrey Six murders is an example of the violence being caused by the business of drugs, not the physical effect of the drug. In my own research several years ago comparing Vancouver and Seattle homicide, I interviewed homicide detectives in both departments. They readily acknowledged that it was not the physical effects of the illegal drugs that caused homicides, but the business of drugs. In fact, the only drug that was consistently noted as producing violence from its consumption was alcohol, particularly among males. As one detective observed at the time, 'but for alcohol and illegal drugs we would largely be out of business!'

An important aspect of the "war on drugs' in the United States is through civil law and processes, such as civil forfeiture and property inspections. Such an approach is used in part to evade the high evidence standards of criminal law and the rights associated with criminal process. In fact, in the United States there are cases of police departments obtaining sizable financial gain through such a process. Unfortunately this has often been to the detriment of civil rights and liberties. The U.S. experience is that the "war on drugs" has greatly intruded upon citizens rights and created many "exceptions" to rights of privacy and security of the person, among other rights.

In a chapter entitled "Civil Responses to Marijuana Grow Ops", the authors provide an excellent overview of the use of distorted claims of the dangers of marijuana grow ops to create new punitive strategies outside the formal scope of the criminal law. For example, exaggerated claims regarding the fire hazards of grow ops led to the B.C. Safety Standards Amendment Act (2006) allowing some municipalities to develop programs using electrical inspections of private residences without a search warrant to detect grow ops. This effort was led by Surrey and has been said to be a great success. B.C. Hydro has been a willing participant and major source of "information" about marijuana grow ops. The book authors note that two RCMP supported studies by Plecas et al were widely quoted in the newspapers and used to justify claims of the dangers of marijuana grow ops. Boyd and Carter point out that the 2005 study report findings do not support the claims made by the authors and RCMP. Using independent data, Boyd and Carter show that the claims are exaggerated.

One program emanating from this approach was the Electrical Fire Safety Initiative (FFSI) which began in Surrey in 2005.

This entailed cooperation between police, firefighters, provincial government, BC Safety Authority and municipal electrical inspectors. By analyzing electrical consumption via BC Hydro or through tips to the police, addresses are identified that are "suspect". Subsequently an investigation of the suspect property and its residents is undertaken. In a 2005 report on the Surrey pilot program Fire Chief Len Garis deemed it a success. Based on the RCMP supported report by Plecas et al, claims were made that grow ops are 24 times more likely to catch fire, but as Boyd and Carter again note, the data are insufficient to support the claim. Further exaggerated claims are reportedly made by Chief Garis about the "grave public safety concerns" surrounding marijuana grow ops, such as bobby traps, violence, organized crime, among others. Boyd and Carter do not contend that these issues do not arise, but that they are very much exaggerated out of proportion to their reality.

Finally, the authors cite a 2009 paper by Chief Garis, Plecas and others which advocates municipalities use civil process and law to address this issues as a public safety concern, not as a criminal concern. It encourages others to lobby politicians to support this type of programs to "weed" out this new public menace. While the propaganda campaign against marijuana grow ops was working in some jurisdictions, others were not interested in this thinly veiled attempt to enforce criminal drug laws and some challenged it for its possible infringement on Charter Rights. Boyd and Carter cite the case of Arkinstall v. City of Surrey as one of he first challenges to the new civil approach to controlling marijuana. The BC Court of Appeal found in 2010 that although conduced under the guise of civil/regulatory law, the inspection infringes section 8 of the Charter of Rights and Freedoms. A couple and their child had their hydro turned off because they refused to comply with the intrusion into their privacy and had to relocate to a hotel. It was disclosed in the case that BC Hydro had forwarded electrical consumption records of over 6000 Surrey properties to authorities, with 1000 flagged for inspection. The property owner is billed for the inspection! A recent challenge to a similar process in Mission has been launched by several residents with the support of the BC Civil Liberties Union. One thing we definitely know as a consequence of the "war on drugs" is that individual rights are increasingly being eroded by government intrusions, often based upon propaganda about the evils of illegal drugs.

In a provocative chapter entitled "Using Children to Promote Increased Regulation", Boyd and Carter detail how media representations of children in grow ops present images of children harmed by the thoughtless, criminal and greedy actions of their parents. This includes harm from mold, carbon monoxide, pesticides, carbon dioxide, ozone exposure and electrocution. They cite an article entitled "Mounties Want Parents Punished for Raising Kids in Grow Ops", stating that 20% of grow ops raided by police have children. Further support of putting children into government care is provided by a quote from police researcher Plecas that stiff jail sentences will act as a deterrent. Again, no independent research is provided. In fact, the history of the past 100 years of criminalization of drugs (including Prohibition) suggests the criminal approach is a largely a failure. Ironically, the authors note that Canada in recent years is adopting the failed policies of the US emphasizing mandatory minimums and increased incarceration, When I moved from Canada to the US in 2007 the US was reaching the height of its get-tough policy, jailing more and more poor, largely non-white, non-violent offenders for drug violations. Now the US is retreating from the failed "war on drugs", reducing mandatory minimums, and moving to a less punitive approach, including legalization of marijuana and widespread medical marijuana. Yet, Canada is going in the opposite direction, adopting many of the failed US policies.

In their last chapter the authors address alternative perspectives. They start out by quoting Canadian drug expert Bruce Alexander: "The biggest cost of the drug war propaganda may be the systematic reduction in people's ability to think intelligently about drugs." They note that the National Anti Drug Strategy Budget for 2012-2017 has a 26% decrease in funding for Community Initiatives and a 35% decrease in Drug Treatment, while there is a 16% increase in RCMP Drug Enforcement, 31% increase for community supervision for Corrections Canada, a 46% increase for the Parole Board of Canada, and increases for Canada Border Services.

There are other options, including harm reduction strategies, which try to minimize the negative effects of not only drug use, but of drug policy. This approach takes more of a treatment/medical approach with services provided and the recognition that drugs will be with us and cannot be eliminated through criminal/punitive approach. The example of contrasts is Vancouver and Surrey. Vancouver has a city strategy of harm reduction with legal injection sites, provision of multiple services to addicts and less reliance on criminal law, particularly regarding marijuana. The 420 celebration in Vancouver acknowledges, like Seattle Hemp Fest, that marijuana law enforcement is a low priority. This would not likely occur in Surrey, given the get-tough approach of the RCMP and city officials. During my 15 years teaching at the University of Calgary I would point out how ideology/philosophy/politics can influence the enforcement of laws. Alberta would always seem to have much higher marijuana arrest rates than BC, although BC has a higher use of marijuana. It is a matter of priorities provincially and in terms of municipalities.

There is a major battle going on now regarding the new law requiring medical marijuana users to buy from government grow ops, not those under current license. Vancouver has announced that it will not crack down on those licensed under previous law, while the RCMP has already seized the first shipments of government grown marijuana for alleged violations. Finally, in a Vancouver Sun Opinion column by Ian Mulgrew, he tells the story of an elderly couple being pursued by the BC Director of Civil Forfeiture for a 2008 offence of growing marijuana for a compassion club![1] As this book shows in vivid detail, propaganda about marijuana and marijuana grow ops has far reaching consequences for all citizens.

Chuck Reasons is a Professor of Law and Justice at Central Washington University. He has published 9 books and many professional articles and book chapters. A 1992 UBC law graduate, he practiced in Vancouver during the 1990's.

---

[1] Ian Mulgrew: Court case provides opportunity for debate about marijuana dispensaries. April 29, 2013. The Vancouver Sun.
http://www.vancouversun.com/health/Mulgrew+Court+case+provides+opportunity+debate+about+marijuana+dispensaries/8312644/story.html

Radical Criminology, an insurgent journal of theory and practice for struggle

Considering contributing to an upcoming issue?

Authors are encouraged to submit articles for publication, directly to our website: **http://journal.radicalcriminology.org**

We are actively seeking marginalized voices, not only in the field of critical criminological scholarship, but also artists, activists, and reviewers. Or, send us a letter!

All academic articles are subject to a blind peer review process. (This does not include "insurgencies," artwork, poetry and book reviews, which will be assessed by our editorial committee.)

Please visit our website for more detailed submission guidelines. (There are no submission nor publication fees.) Create a 'reader' and 'author' account there now...

We use the Public Knowledge Project's 'open journal' online submission system (http://pkp.sfu.ca/ojs), which allows authors to submit papers via the Web. This system speeds up the submission and review process, and allows you to view the status of your paper online.

Artwork, poetic submissions, and notes on insurgencies can also be posted to our website, e-mailed to <editors@radicalcriminology.org> or send us mail at:

Radical Criminology,
ATTN: Jeff Shantz, Dept. of Criminology,
Kwantlen Polytechnic University
12666 72nd Ave,
Surrey, B.C. V3W 2M8

(and on twitter............................find us @critcrim)

ISSN: 1929-7904

"... more hopefully, there is the real possibility that new and more effective approaches will be developed, refined, and pursued. Forgotten voices and lost wisdom will once again be engaged in meaningful ways. This is already being realized in the widespread, and growing, engagement with anarchism, indigenous thinking, radical unionism, syndicalism, and horizontalism and direct action."

-- from the Manifesto, issue #1

Radical Criminology
an insurgent journal

download freely the entire issue as a PDF
or order affordable print copies to be mailed to you...

radicalcriminology.org /issue1

radicalcriminology.org /issue2

radicalcriminology.org /issue3

... then login to our website to create an "author" account, and submit to an upcoming issue! We are now seeking articles, artwork, insurgencies & book reviews. **Upcoming issue featuring** *PUBLIC CRIMINOLOGIES*

//journal.radicalcriminology.org

radicalcrim@riseup.net   twitter: @critcrim

an **open access journal!**

punctum books * brooklyn, ny

Made in the USA
Charleston, SC
03 November 2014